Praise for Dian
The Comp

Diana Glyer's is the best account we have, not only of the friendship between Lewis and Tolkien, and the other Inklings, but also of the practical help and support they offered to each other: as critics, editors, collaborators, motivators. For both Lewis and Tolkien, the spark came from flint and steel, and Diana Glyer shows the many ways they struck it. Her book is an indispensable account not just of friendship, but also of the paths of creativity.

    Tom Shippey, author of *The Road to Middle-earth* and *J.R.R. Tolkien, Author of the Century*

This is an indispensable contribution to the study of what may fairly be called the 20th century's most influential group of writers.

    Michael Ward, author of *Planet Narnia*

I love *The Company They Keep*. I quote it all the time for its insights into the friendship of these important authors.

    Alister McGrath, author of *C.S. Lewis—A Life: Eccentric Genius, Reluctant Prophet*

Reading the remarkable *The Company They Keep: C.S. Lewis and J.R.R. Tolkien as Writers in Community* proves that Diana Pavlac Glyer has vaulted into the company of the very best thinkers and writers on the Inklings.

    REVIEW: *Mythlore: A Journal of J.R.R. Tolkien, C.S. Lewis, Charles Williams, and Mythopoeic Literature*

This is an impressive piece of work, and it has the great merit of being both authentically scholarly and entertaining at the same time. Just start reading. You will find yourself drawn straightaway into an account of things that (I'll wager) would have the Inklings themselves turning the pages.

    Thomas T. Howard, author of *The Novels of Charles Williams* and *Evangelical Is Not Enough*

Glyer concludes that writers don't create in a vacuum; every artist's work is inevitably embedded in the work of others. Community doesn't stifle creativity or individual expression. Rather, it fertilizes and nurtures it. For anyone interested in how a favorite book came to be, and especially for artists exploring their own craft, *The Company They Keep* is a must read.

John Adcox, author of *The Widening Gyre* and *Raven Wakes the World*

The Company They Keep is a wonder of a book. In a relatively short treatment, it manages to be scholarly enough to satisfy the most meticulous Inklings scholar yet lively enough to engage readers who have only a passing interest in Lewis or Tolkien. It successfully addresses the needs of both scholars in composition studies and teachers of writing as they seek to understand how writers groups work, and how to best employ these techniques to improve writing. And the book will appeal to the wider group of people who hope to become more creative by using exemplary role models. This book deserves to be read and incorporated into our classroom techniques. It deserves to be assigned as a text to our students as they become better writers. And it deserves to be enjoyed as the insightful read that it is.

REVIEW: *Pedagogy: Critical Approaches to Teaching Literature, Language, Composition and Culture*

Glyer's prose is not only a delight to read, but it is also full of keen analysis and valuable insight into the nature of the Inklings' complicated interrelationship. *The Company They Keep* is truly an important contribution to Inklings studies as well as an excellent example of how literary critics can approach the thorny issue of influence in a careful, balanced way.

REVIEW: *Mythprint: The Monthly Bulletin of the Mythopoeic Society*

If you thought you knew everything there was to know about the Inklings, this book will change your mind. There's still more to be discovered about how they interacted. Glyer's style is brisk, clear and engaging. But beyond that, her insights into the Inklings are exceptional.

TOP REVIEW: Scribblerworks.com

Reading it was simply pure enjoyment!—diving into another and delightful world. It is simply a tremendous reading experience.

Bruce G. Charlton, M.D., editor-in-chief, *Medical Hypotheses*

Glyer sees the hidden currents that serve as influences among writers, which makes this book as much a study about the act of writing in community as it is about the Inklings themselves. In other words, one need not be interested in the Inklings to be drawn in. It's a fascinating case-study in group dynamics and the creative process, and because the two main subjects of the book, Tolkien and Lewis, also happen to be two of the past century's most important writers, the book serves as a lens into the mechanism of genius as well.

REVIEW: *APU Research Reporter*

The beauty of this book lies in the clarity and eloquence of the author's prose. It is one of those extraordinary academic works that is actually easy and enjoyable to read. Whether you are a new fan of these authors or you have been studying them for years, you will find plenty to enjoy within the pages of this book.

REVIEW: www.theOneRing.com

Here's the thing. Glyer obviously did her homework. I see many familiar quotes, always used in the right place, never distorted or misemployed. She's also found some good stuff that I've never read, or haven't read for years and years. She has an impressive bibliography (anyone wishing to study the Inklings ought to buy the book for the bibliography in and of itself) and superlative notes. But here's the real appeal: the engaging, lucid, crystal-clear writing style that graces her steel-strong research.

Sherwood Smith, author of *Inda*, *The Fox*, and *Wren to the Rescue*

I found myself captured by her engaging writing style, the breadth of her research, and the cogency of her argument. Her work will influence the texture of Inklings scholarship for years to come. It's good, very good indeed.

Verlyn Flieger, coeditor (with Douglas Anderson and Michael Drout) of *Tolkien Studies*

The Company They Keep certainly contributes to the ongoing conversation about Lewis, Tolkien, and the others, but rather than being an addition to that conversation, this book will undoubtedly redirect its course. From now on, the rest of us will talk about these pivotal writers and scholars differently. Glyer has taken these writers—and by extension all artists and scholars—out of their solitary towers and placed them back in the community where they belong.

David Esselstrom, chair, Department of English, Azusa Pacific University

Diana Glyer has crafted the most intimate, clear, authoritative study yet of the Inklings, the famous Oxford writers' clique that included, among others, J.R.R. Tolkien and C.S. Lewis. By bringing the group's dynamics openly before us, she enables us to encounter the customs, personalities, and writings of its authors. It is really quite a stunning achievement.

REVIEW: *The Lion and the Unicorn*

Bandersnatch

Bandersnatch

C. S. Lewis, J. R. R. Tolkien, and
the Creative Collaboration of the Inklings

Diana Pavlac Glyer

Illustrated by James A. Owen

Black Squirrel Books™ 🐿™ Kent, Ohio

Publisher's Note: *Bandersnatch: C. S. Lewis, J. R. R. Tolkien, and the Creative Collaboration of the Inklings* is abridged and adapted from *The Company They Keep: C. S. Lewis and J. R. R. Tolkien as Writers in Community* (Kent State University Press, 2007). Readers interested in a more thorough and scholarly treatment of this subject are encouraged to seek out that earlier volume.

BLACK SQUIRREL BOOKS™ 🐿️™
Frisky, industrious black squirrels are a familiar sight on the Kent State University campus and the inspiration for Black Squirrel Books™, a trade imprint of The Kent State University Press
www.KentStateUniversityPress.com

Library of Congress Cataloging-in-Publication Data
Names: Glyer, Diana Pavlac, author. | Owen, James A., illustrator.
Title: Bandersnatch : C. S. Lewis, J. R. R. Tolkien, and the creative collaboration of the Inklings / Diana Pavlac Glyer ; iIllustrated by James A. Owen.
Description: Kent, Ohio : The Kent State University Press, 2016. | Includes bibliographical references and index.
Identifiers: LCCN 2015036099 | ISBN 9781606352762 (pbk. : alk. paper) ∞
Subjects: LCSH: Inklings (Group of writers) | Creation (Literary, artistic, etc.) | Lewis, C. S. (Clive Staples), 1898-1963--Criticism and interpretation. | Tolkien, J. R. R. (John Ronald Reuel), 1892-1973--Criticism and interpretation. | Literature and society--England--History--20th century.
Classification: LCC PR478.I54 G59 2016 | DDC 820.9/00912--dc23
LC record available at http://lccn.loc.gov/2015036099

22 21   5

To Sierra Grace,
the joy of my heart

"You see, a minute goes by so fearfully quick. You might as well try to stop a Bandersnatch."
—Lewis Carroll (in *Through the Looking Glass* 1871)

"No-one ever influenced Tolkien—you might as well try to influence a bandersnatch."
—C. S. Lewis (in a letter to a reader 1959)

Contents

Illustrations

Acknowledgments

This is a book about collaboration, and from start to finish, it was created collaboratively. I remain convinced that books should have a list of credits at the end, just like movies. We need more capacious ways to talk about what collaboration looks like and why it matters. But that is not the custom among writers and publishers. Perhaps some day it will be.

James Artimus Owen: Thanks for catching the vision and flinging yourself into the thick of this creative collaboration. Wasn't it fun?

Team Bandersnatch—Josie Zimmerman and Danielle Coleman—I love you guys. Thanks for meeting every week (for more than a year!) to eat chocolate and work on this manuscript. You believed in the work when I was not so sure. How can I ever thank you?

Bethany Wagner, Josh B. Long, David Bratman, Alene Campbell-Langdell, Melissa Campbell-Langdell, Roger White, Joel Heck, Lynn Maudlin, Barbara Nicolosi, Nancy Brashear, Christine Kern, and Kelly Lauer read the manuscript and made suggestions and issued stern warnings. If I had been a better listener, this would have been a better book. Though I intend to deny it, there are those who have whispered that the "Bandersnatch" referred to in these pages would be me.

Primary research is possible only to the extent that there are devoted librarians who labor to make rare books, letters, diaries, manuscripts, and other treasures available. I would like to thank The Marion E. Wade Center, Wheaton College, Wheaton, Illinois, and everyone associated with it for offering a wealth of resources and unflagging support. Special thanks must be given for the Clyde S. Kilby Grant (1997), which provided the practical help needed to make this research possible. I am also so grateful for the staff at the Bodleian Library, Oxford. Ann Wilson tracked down details. Roger White, Curator of the Inklings Collection at Azusa Pacific University, not only provided a wealth of materials but also spent long hours conspiring to track down tiny, tiny details that provided the keys to solving the big mysteries.

Sometimes technology is a wonderful thing. Friends on Facebook commiserated, prayed, ate chocolate (to show their solidarity), and listened to me whine and worry. You. Are. Awesome. A special shout-out to Jeff Goins and the members of Tribe Writers. Stay on track. Don't lose heart. Do the work. Then get up tomorrow and do it again.

I am grateful to Joel Heck, whose Lewis chronology serves as an anchor to all conversation about Lewis and his life and work, and Wayne Hammond and Christina Scull, whose Tolkien chronology anchors all conversation about Tolkien.

I also want to thank Steve Laube (you give me courage); Andrew Lazo (you kept the faith until I could believe again); Linda Sherman Spitser (you are my guardian angel); and the members of K.A.M.M. (you are vast and brilliant). You make all the difference.

I received generous support from the administration at Azusa Pacific University, Azusa, California. I would especially like to thank David Esselstrom, David Weeks, and Jennifer Walsh for supporting my work on this manuscript.

I remain indebted to David Bratman, who has been resonator, opponent, editor, collaborator, and referent at every stage of my research and writing about the Inklings. Special thanks for compiling an index that is not only accurate and comprehensive but genuinely useful. A good index is a work of art, a kind of miracle.

Prayer warriors from the Niños have met twice a month for nearly 20 years: You have undergirded every single step of progress that I have made. Collaboration in community. Without you, there would be no books.

Many fine scholars are dedicated to the study of Lewis, Tolkien, and the Inklings, and you have enriched my life by writing books, organizing conferences, presenting papers, giving advice, answering questions, correcting my errors, offering insight, and providing encouragement. I am blessed by the company I keep, and I marvel at the privilege of having a seat at the table.

This book is dedicated to Sierra Grace, because she liked the title, and because she was both cheerful and helpful as she put up with the daily bother of yet another book.

Bandersnatch

C. S. Lewis at Magdalen College

CHAPTER ONE

Dusting for Fingerprints

 I had been at it for about five weeks. It was Thursday, but you could hardly tell. My routine continued day after day, pretty much the same. Wake up in my hotel room. Have coffee and a granola bar for breakfast. Look over yesterday's notes and update my to-do list. Walk to the Wade Center, arriving just as they unlocked the doors. Sit down at a long wooden table, pull out my pencil, and start shuffling through loose sheaves of papers, searching for some shred of evidence.

I was on a mission. Years before, when I was still in high school, I discovered *The Lord of the Rings,* and I was quite simply enchanted. Hungry for more books like it, I stumbled upon C. S. Lewis and *Out of the Silent Planet.* And soon after, I discovered that J. R. R. Tolkien and C. S. Lewis were friends. Both worked at Oxford University. They founded a writing group known as the Inklings.

When I discovered the Inklings, I was only 16 years old, and I wanted to know the answers to two simple questions. What did these writers talk about when they met to discuss their works in progress? And what difference did these conversations make to the books they were writing?

It seemed to me that it would be really easy to find the answers. I spent years reading everything I could get my hands on: everything written about the Inklings and everything written by them. While lots of books talked about the Inklings in general terms, no one offered me a close-up, fly-on-the-wall perspective. No one seemed to be able to tell me exactly what they talked about or what difference it made.

About this time, one of my mentors got a whiff of what I was up to. He took me aside and said with all the kindness he could muster, "Here's what you need to do: Give this up. You will never find what you're looking for. Everyone knows the Inklings influenced each other, but you are never going to find enough evidence to prove it. And I don't want you wasting your life looking for something that just isn't there."

I cried for a week. No, more than that. I was a beginner, and he was a senior scholar. And he was my mentor, my teacher, and my friend.

Once I calmed down, I made a decision. Maybe he was right. Maybe I would never find the answers to my questions. But that didn't matter. I was going to keep looking anyway. And I was going to follow the evidence wherever it might lead.

That's how (years later) I found myself spending the summer at the Wade Center, a research library in Wheaton, Illinois. I'd exhausted every published resource, so I needed to dig into the primary documents. I wanted to read their letters and diaries to find out what the Inklings themselves had to say about the group. I wanted to study the manuscript pages, searching for evidence that might be hidden in the margins.

Then, on a Thursday in July, I was reading through the letters of J. R. R. Tolkien. I was tracking his progress on *The Hobbit* and *The Lord of the Rings:*

January 4, 1937: Tolkien has recovered from the flu and is redoing the illustrations for *The Hobbit.*

September 21, 1937: *The Hobbit* is published. The reviews are glowing, the sales are brisk, and as a result, the readers are restless. The book is selling so well that Stanley Unwin does what publishers always do: he demands a sequel.

October 15, 1937: Tolkien says no. He complains, "I cannot think of anything more to say about hobbits."

December 16, 1937: Tolkien relents. He promises to try to write something more about hobbits and manages to draft three chapters of a new story.

March 4, 1938: He shows the early chapters to C. S. Lewis and also to his son Christopher Tolkien. They like it very much.

April and May 1938: Unwin keeps pestering Tolkien for more chapters. Tolkien just ignores him.

June 4, 1938: Tolkien sends Unwin a brief progress report. He hems and haws and finally confesses, "I have not had a chance to touch any story-writing since the Christmas vacation."

Christmas vacation? That means he hasn't touched the book in more than five months. If that sounds like bad news for a publisher, the rest of the report is even worse. Tolkien tells Unwin that instead of drafting more material, he has decided to start over and rewrite the first three chapters.

What motivated Tolkien to go back and start the whole thing over again? He says he has been thinking about the "excellent criticism" he has received from his readers. C. S. Lewis is one of those readers, and Lewis has complained that there is too much dialogue, too much chatter, too much silly "hobbit talk." According to Lewis, all this dialogue is dragging down the story line.

Tolkien grumbles. "The trouble is that 'hobbit talk' amuses me . . . more than adventures; but I must curb this severely."

Whoa. I had been spending day after day in the library, sitting on a wooden chair, turning pages, jotting notes. Then I ran smack into this: primary evidence from Tolkien's letters that Lewis was involved with the first draft of the very first chapters of *The Lord of the Rings*. Lewis read the chapters, liked the story, and encouraged Tolkien. He also took the time to critique it and make specific suggestions for its improvement. And Tolkien sounds like he is taking this feedback very seriously.

This was the breakthrough I was looking for. I was thrilled by these discoveries, but they just led me to the Next Big Question: What happened next? Did Tolkien actually follow Lewis's advice?

To find the answer, I turned my attention to the manuscripts themselves. In this case, the detective work was pretty straightforward: find a copy of Tolkien's early draft, and then compare it side-by-side with his revised version.

Take a look. Here's an excerpt, a short section from Book One of *The Lord of the Rings*. At this point in the story, three Hobbits named Bingo, Odo, and Frodo are sorting through their travel gear and stuffing it into heavy backpacks as they prepare to leave Hobbiton behind and begin their adventures.

Tolkien's Early Draft:

"Be kind to a poor ruined Hobbit!" laughed Bingo. "I shall be thin as a willow-wand, I'm sure, before a week is out. But now what about it? Let's have a council! What shall we do first?"

"I thought that was settled," said Odo. "Surely we have got to pick up Marmaduke first of all?"

"O yes! I didn't mean that," said Bingo. "I meant: what about this evening? Shall we walk a little or a lot? All night or not at all?"

"We'd better find some snug corner in a haystack, or somewhere, and turn in soon," said Odo. "We shall do more tomorrow, if we start fresh."

"Let's put a bit of the road behind us to-night," said Frodo. "I want to get away from Hobbiton. Besides it's jolly under the stars, and cool."

"I vote for Frodo," said Bingo. And so they started, shouldering their packs, and swinging their stout sticks. They went very quietly over fields and along hedgerows and the borders of coppices, until night fell. In their dark grey cloaks they were invisible without the help of any magic rings, and since they were all hobbits, they made no noise that even hobbits would hear (or indeed even wild creatures in the woods and fields).

Tolkien's Revised Version:

"Be kind to a poor old hobbit!" laughed Frodo. "I shall be as thin as a willow-wand, I'm sure, before I get to Buckland. But I was talking nonsense. I suspect you have taken more than your share, Sam, and I shall look into it at our next packing." He picked up his stick again. "Well, we all like walking in the dark," he said, "so let's put some miles behind us before bed."

For a short way they followed the lane westwards. Then leaving it they turned left and took quietly to the fields again. They went in single file along hedgerows and the borders of coppices, and night fell dark about them. In their dark cloaks they were as invisible as if they all had magic rings. Since they were all hobbits, and were trying to be silent, they made no noise that even hobbits would hear. Even the wild things in the fields and woods hardly noticed their passing.

Tolkien completely changes the names and relationships of these characters. In the first draft, the story centers on a hobbit named Bingo, who sets out with two companions (Odo Took and Frodo Took). As Tolkien revises, Bingo becomes Frodo, and he is joined by his friends Sam and Pippin. (I wonder—would *The Lord of the Rings* have been nearly so popular if the main character had been called Bingo all along?)

But more than just names have been transformed. The revised version is shorter and much clearer, too. It takes Tolkien 211 words to cover this material in the draft, but only 162 words in the revised version. What's even more striking is how the proportions of narrative and dialogue have changed. When Tolkien rewrote this material, he cut nearly half of the dialogue.

Tolkien's work in these paragraphs is typical of his work on all three of these beginning chapters. Page after page, he cuts out long conversations, and he picks up the action. Even though he personally prefers a story with much more "hobbit talk," he bows to his critics and creates a tale with much less.

He also makes small but elegant refinements throughout the pages. While the biggest change is in the proportions of dialogue and action and the way that changes the pace of the story, I can't help noticing how much better the style is, how much smoother the sentences are, how much better they sound.

There are many other changes in the various drafts of the manuscript. Tolkien revises and improves his material constantly, and many different readers offer input along the way. As I did my work, it was tempting to try to document all of these changes and chase down all of these influencers. But I wanted to find out what the Inklings said, and I wanted to figure out what difference it made. So I tried to stay focused. In looking at these early chapters, I traced the impact of one specific comment. Lewis told Tolkien to cut down the dialogue. Did he? Yes, without question. The changes in the manuscript show he did. And the timing of events shows that Tolkien was responding to Lewis's comments when he did it. And the unfolding story suggests that Tolkien kept this advice in mind as he wrote the following chapters.

Discoveries like that sustained me. I traveled and read and researched and wrote. I presented sections of my findings at conferences. And I dug deeper, always going back to the primary documents. I was privileged to correspond with Christopher Tolkien, the last living member of the Inklings. I was honored by the patience and kindness he showed in answering my questions and verifying my hunches.

As I learned about the Inklings, something else began to dawn on me, something wholly unexpected. Something bigger. I wasn't prepared for just how important this group was, how essential it had become to the work of these writers. I thought that being an Inkling was probably helpful and encouraging. But I was starting to see that the group was, somehow, necessary.

Why was this such a surprise? I had tried working collaboratively, mostly when I was in school. It had not proved helpful. One person (usually me) ended up doing all the work while everyone else took the credit. I also remembered participating in committees at work, and more often than not, the whole thing was frustrating. Instead of making progress, very little was accomplished. Instead of enhancing productivity, it felt like a waste of my time.

But when I read about the Inklings, one thing was certain: Much of what they accomplished was the direct result of this group. How was that possible? What was I missing?

I had a hunch that maybe they saw collaboration in a different way. Maybe they had a bigger picture of what it involved. When I started my research, I just wanted to know what their collaborative process looked like. Now I began to wonder if there were larger lessons here, ones that could make a difference in the projects I was working on, in the breakthroughs I was seeking.

I spent 23 years sifting through letters and studying drafts. I presented my findings in a book called *The Company They Keep: C. S. Lewis and J. R. R. Tolkien as Writers in Community*. That book changed the way we talk about these authors because it showed how much the Inklings influenced each other as they worked together week after week.

The Company They Keep is a book for scholars, detailing the threads of influence that connected all of the members of this writers group. As one reviewer noted, it is accessible and lively but, nonetheless, it is fundamentally academic in nature.

Several years ago, it occurred to me that the stories of Lewis and Tolkien and their collaboration should be presented for a wider audience. *Bandersnatch* is a new version of their story. It is my hope that it will enchant any reader who loves these authors and wants to learn more about how they worked together.

DOING WHAT THEY DID: Evidence of creative breakthrough is found in unlikely places: a quick note, an offhand remark, a journal entry, or a formal letter. We gather the scraps, and we piece them together the best we can. The fact is, creativity itself is a messy business. We want to think of it as linear and efficient, but in actuality, it is full of false starts, dead ends, long hours, setbacks, discouragement, and frustrations. Knowing that it works this way can help us be more patient with our own untidy processes.

Hugo Dyson at The Eagle and Child

CHAPTER TWO

"An Unexpected Party"

 C. S. Lewis and J. R. R. Tolkien are remembered as writers of fantasy, but both men made their living teaching English at Oxford University. They met for the first time at a faculty meeting on the 11th of May, 1926. Lewis's first impression of Tolkien wasn't exactly favorable. In his diary, he describes Tolkien as "a smooth, pale, fluent little chap." Then he adds, "No harm in him: only needs a smack or so."

It got worse. As Lewis and Tolkien got to know each other, it became clear that they had a number of serious disagreements. They had different interests and personalities. They came from different religious traditions. And they had different academic specialties. Lewis was an expert in literature and philosophy; Tolkien was a philologist, an expert in languages. He loved Old Norse and Anglo-Saxon. Lewis said that meeting Tolkien triggered two of his childhood prejudices. He explains, "At my first coming into the world I had been (implicitly) warned never to trust a [Catholic], and at my first coming into the English Faculty (explicitly) never to trust a philologist. Tolkien was both."

Within months of Lewis and Tolkien's first meeting, the faculty at Oxford became entrenched in a bitter argument about which courses should be required for students studying in the English School. Lewis and Tolkien found themselves on opposite sides of the debate. Tolkien believed the English curriculum should be based on close study of ancient and medieval texts and their languages. He thought that if students were given a solid foundation, they could read the full range of modern texts on their own. Lewis also loved ancient literature, but he believed students would benefit more from a broad survey of both ancient and modern texts.

Tolkien was prepared to fight energetically for his curriculum. His approach was strategic: he decided the best way to win support for his point of view would be to foster a love for mythology and ancient languages among his colleagues. So he founded a club he called the Kolbítar (literally "the Coalbiters"), adopting an Old Norse word for "old cronies who sit round the fire so close that they look as if they were biting the coals." They met each week to read Icelandic poems and stories. They translated them bit by bit, as much as each person could manage in turn.

Lewis was immediately drawn in. For him, the chance to join the circle was the fulfillment of his love for Norse mythology and his interest in Odin, Freya, and Loki. He was only nine years old when he first discovered these stories and was "uplifted into huge regions of northern sky" that he "desired with almost sickening intensity." At twenty-eight, he was still unabashed in his enthusiasm for these ancient texts: "It is an exciting experience, when I remember my first passion for things Norse under the initiation of Longfellow. . . . It seemed impossible then that I shd. ever come to read these things in the original."

The Kolbítar met regularly, working their way through ancient sagas and thrilling over both the literature and the language. Despite their initial suspicion and professional conflicts, Lewis and Tolkien discovered they had significant common ground. They gravitated towards each other because they shared an interest in what they called "northernness," the vast skies, icy landscapes, and heroic tempers of the ancient Vikings. As they talked together, Lewis was slowly won over to Tolkien's view of the English curriculum. And as they worked side by side, they forged a solid friendship. E. L. Edmonds, a student at Oxford, remembers, "It was very obvious that [Lewis and Tolkien] were great friends—indeed, they were like two young bear cubs sometimes, just happily quipping with one another."

Elves and Men

This change from suspicion to friendship happened as they worked side by side, pursuing a mutual interest. Another change occurred in December of 1929, when Tolkien decided to show Lewis the draft of a poem he had been working on.

The Lay of Leithian describes a mortal man named Beren who falls in love with a beautiful elf named Lúthien Tinúviel. The poem recounts one of the most personal and significant stories in all of his created mythology. Lewis took it home and read it eagerly. The next day, he responded with a brief note, filled with praise: "I can quite honestly say that it is ages since I have had an evening of such delight: and the personal interest of reading a friend's work had very little to do with it. I should have enjoyed it just as well as if I'd picked it up in a bookshop, by an unknown author."

As he read the long narrative poem, Lewis was struck by two qualities in particular. He admired the realism of Tolkien's sub-created world, the depth and detail of Middle-earth. He also praised the mythical value of the story, the way the events were good in themselves and yet also suggested deeper layers of meaning to the reader.

But Lewis ends his letter on an ominous note, promising, "Detailed criticisms (including grumbles at individual lines) will follow." A second letter, full of "criticisms" and "grumbles," arrived some weeks later. Lewis questioned large, conceptual matters. He quibbled about small word choices. He requested specific revisions. He even rewrote entire sections of the poem himself.

Tolkien was as cheered by this careful critique as he had been by the lavish praise. More than anything else, it meant he had found someone who understood his work and was enthusiastic enough about it to give it a close, attentive reading. Although Tolkien did not agree with all of Lewis's comments, he did revise the poem extensively, responding to most of Lewis's suggestions in one way or another. Chapter 5 describes some of these important changes. In sharing this poem, Tolkien had taken a substantial risk, and Lewis had offered a generous, detailed response.

Lewis took the next step and shared some poems of his own. At this point in his life, Lewis saw himself primarily as a poet, and he fully expected that his most significant achievement would be to make his mark as a great poet. Owen Barfield, a friend from their undergraduate days, declared, "At that time, if you thought of Lewis, you automatically thought of poetry."

Tolkien commented extensively on Lewis's poems, offering both praise and criticism. It wasn't long before it became a regular custom for Tolkien and Lewis to meet together in Lewis's rooms at Magdalen College on Monday mornings to read and critique one another's work. Lewis declared that this regular meeting time was "one of the pleasantest spots in the week."

True Myth

Lewis's interaction with Tolkien affected more than just his writing; it led to a transformation of his faith. Lewis had accepted Christianity as a child, but later abandoned God entirely. In 1916, he explained his position to his friend Arthur Greeves:

> You ask me my religious views: you know, I think, that I believe in no religion. There is absolutely no proof for any of them, and from a philosophical standpoint Christianity is not even the best. All religions, that is, all mythologies to give them their proper name are merely man's own invention—Christ as much as Loki. Primitive man found himself surrounded by all sorts of terrible things he didn't understand—thunder, pestilence, snakes etc: what more natural than to suppose that these were animated by evil spirits trying to torture him. These he kept off by cringing to them, singing songs and making sacrifices etc. Gradually from being mere nature-spirits these supposed being[s] were elevated into more elaborate ideas, such as the old gods: and when man became more refined he pretended that these spirits were good as well as powerful.
>
> Thus religion, that is to say mythology grew up.

As a teenager, Lewis dismissed all religions with this neat and tidy explanation: primitive man simply invented religion in a misguided attempt to make sense of the dangers he saw in the natural world.

But as the years went by, Lewis found it increasingly difficult to remain an atheist, in part because he kept meeting intelligent, articulate men who turned out to be Christians. Lewis became friends with Nevill Coghill, "one of the best known and best loved men in Oxford." Coghill was a man of warmth, chivalry, honor, and "gentilesse." Lewis notes, "One could imagine him fighting a duel." They first met as students in a literature class. Despite a promising beginning, Lewis was dismayed when he discovered that even though Coghill was "clearly the most intelligent and best-informed man in that class," he was a Christian and "a thoroughgoing supernaturalist."

Shortly after, two of Lewis's most important college friends—Cecil Harwood and Owen Barfield—rejected atheism and became followers of Anthroposophy, believers in an objective, accessible spiritual world. This seriously upset Lewis, who writes,

> I was hideously shocked. Everything that I had laboured so hard to expel from my own life seemed to have flared up and met me in my best friends. Not only my best friends but those whom I would have thought safest; the one so immovable, the other brought up in a free-thinking family and so immune from all "superstition" that he had hardly heard of Christianity itself until he went to school.

Though he was distressed by the religious conversions of his friends, it upset Lewis even more to find that many of the authors he loved best were also devout men of faith. He was unsettled when he realized that knowing God was absolutely central to the thought of George MacDonald, G. K. Chesterton, Samuel Johnson, Edmund Spenser, John Milton, William Langland, John Donne, and Thomas Browne. He says the most alarming influence of all came from George Herbert. Even Plato, Aeschylus, and Virgil challenged him with their easy acceptance of the idea of a supernatural reality. The assault, it seemed, was relentless. Tongue in cheek, he writes, "Really, a young Atheist cannot guard his faith too carefully. Dangers lie in wait for him on every side."

The "dangers" became increasingly insistent. In a letter to Barfield, Lewis expressed the gnawing sense that something was closing in on him. "Terrible things are happening to me," he writes, and he expresses concern that God seemed to be "taking the offensive." He continues, miserably, "You'd better come on Monday at the latest or I may have entered a monastery."

Eventually, the old belief system that Lewis had constructed with such great care simply collapsed. In an often-quoted passage, he writes, "I gave in, and admitted that God was God, and knelt and prayed: perhaps, that night, the most dejected and reluctant convert in all England."

His conversion to Theism, to belief in God, took place in June 1930. More than a year later, Lewis became a Christian. There were many factors that contributed to his commitment to Christ, but the turning point came in September of 1931, following a long talk with two of his friends. One was J. R. R. Tolkien. The other was Hugo Dyson.

Dyson was a man of unusually bold and lively character. He has been described as "a man who gives the impression of being made of quick silver: he pours himself into a room on a cataract of words and gestures, and you are caught up in the stream—but after the first plunge, it is exhilarating." Dyson's strong personality could be quite destructive, as we will see in chapter 4. Still, Lewis admired Dyson for his fine mind, vibrant character, and merry laugh. Lewis's descriptions generally emphasize his vivacity and quickness of speech. He also pays Dyson the high compliment of calling him "a man who really loves truth."

On 19 September 1931, Dyson, Tolkien, and Lewis had dinner at Magdalen, then went out onto Addison's Walk and talked late into the night. Lewis was confronted about his old anti-Christian biases and encouraged to consider Christianity as a true myth:

> Now what Dyson and Tolkien showed me was this: that if I met the idea of sacrifice in a Pagan story I didn't mind it at all: again, that if I met the idea of a god sacrificing himself to himself . . . I liked it very much and was mysteriously moved by it: again, that the idea of the dying and reviving god (Balder, Adonis, Bacchus) similarly moved me provided I met it anywhere *except* in the Gospels. The reason was that in Pagan stories I was prepared to feel the myth as profound and suggestive of meanings beyond my grasp even tho' I could not say in cold prose "what it meant".
>
> Now the story of Christ is simply a true myth: a myth working on

us in the same way as the others, but with this tremendous difference that *it really happened.*

Lewis's commitment to Christ became the central fact of his life. And the turning point was this specific conversation. Lewis writes, "Dyson and Tolkien were the immediate human causes of my own conversion."

Warnie Comes Home

While C. S. Lewis was beginning his career as an academic at Oxford, his older brother, Warren Hamilton Lewis, was half a world away, serving as an officer at a Royal Army Service Corps depot in China. Warren Lewis decided on a military career when he was seventeen. He served for more than 20 years in supplies and transport. Historian Richard C. West explains that even though this assignment may seem rather tame, it was "dangerous enough work in wartime when being strafed by enemy planes, and always entailing responsibility for thousands of soldiers." Major Lewis served in England, France, China, and West Africa.

The two brothers were uncommonly close all their lives. As children, they played together, wrote stories of imagined worlds together, and painted pictures and drew maps in creative interaction. Chapter 6 offers more details of this early collaboration.

When their mother died of cancer in 1908, they became even closer, like "two frightened urchins huddled for warmth in a bleak world." Both boys attended Wynyard School and Malvern College. And both were tutored by William T. Kirkpatrick, who said of Warren Lewis, "He is one of the nicest, best tempered, personally amiable boys I have ever met. To live in the house with him is a pleasure, and no one could sit working along with him so long as I have done without developing an affection for him."

Warren Lewis, also known as "Warnie," was a warm and gentle man and a gifted writer. After he retired, he came to live in Oxford. He and his brother bought a house together, and Warnie was eager to find some new challenge. He decided to edit the Lewis family papers, a process we'll consider in chapter 3. He loved the work, calling it "one of the most engrossing tasks I have ever undertaken."

He spent most weekdays working on this project, researching and writing in Lewis's rooms at Magdalen College. On Monday mornings, it was only natural for him to join his brother "Jack" and friend Tolkien for conversation and critique. Then the three of them would head over to the Eastgate Hotel for lunch and a pint of beer.

The Inklings

It was a small beginning—no big plans, no particular agenda. Just a few writers gathering each week for encouragement and conversation. To the extent that there is one critical moment of origin of the group, it would be the 6th of December, 1929, the day Tolkien made the courageous decision to share his created mythology with Lewis. From there, a more regular pattern developed as Tolkien and Lewis began scheduling time specifically to read and critique each other's work. Their meetings received a boost in 1931, when Lewis renewed his Christian faith, and another when Warren Lewis retired in 1932, moved to Oxford, and joined them.

Then the group began to grow. They called themselves the Inklings, and the name tells us something about the nature of the group. It was not a literary society, nor was it a forum for general discussion, although those kinds of groups are quite common in Oxford. It was more focused. This was a meeting of working writers. Members brought drafts they were working on. They read them aloud, received comments, and revised their work in response to what they heard.

As Tolkien points out, the name is "a pleasantly ingenious pun," referring to those who "dabble in ink." It also suggests people "with vague or half-formed intimations and ideas." The manuscripts they brought to meetings were often rough drafts in their earliest stages. They came ready to make significant changes as they responded to criticism and feedback from the members. When Tolkien wrote a story about a fictional writing group much like the Inklings, he called it "The Notion Club," reinforcing the view that they were working with "notions":

fleeting ideas, or tentative drafts in progress. There is evidence of extensive revision to these early drafts, as we will see in later chapters.

All in all, nineteen men are considered members of the Inklings. They are Owen Barfield, J. A. W. Bennett, David Cecil, Nevill Coghill, James Dundas-Grant, Hugo Dyson, Adam Fox, Colin Hardie, Robert E. "Humphrey" Havard, C. S. Lewis, Warren Lewis, Gervase Mathew, R. B. McCallum, C. E. Stevens, Christopher Tolkien, J. R. R. Tolkien, John Wain, Charles Williams, and C. L. Wrenn.

The group was large and loosely knit, but a typical Thursday night meeting was fairly small. On average, six or seven men would show up. Four of the Inklings—the two Lewis brothers, Tolkien, and Dr. Havard—attended the meetings most faithfully.

Dr. Robert E. Havard met Lewis when he was called to Lewis's home, "the Kilns," to treat him for an attack of the flu. According to Havard, "On my first visit we spent some five minutes discussing his influenza, which was very straightforward, and then half an hour or more in a discussion of ethics and philosophy." This is not surprising: Havard was "well-read and keenly interested in the processes of literature and in theology."

Havard reports that shortly after his first visit to the Kilns, Lewis invited him to come and join the Inklings, describing it as "a group of us who meet on Thursday evenings and read papers and discuss them." As a physician, Havard might seem to be an unlikely participant in this group of Oxford literary men. But Havard was a skilled writer. He coauthored and published a number of medical research papers, along with several important memoirs. He had a talent for giving feedback: Havard made detailed comments on *The Problem of Pain* and offered significant encouragement as Lewis was writing The Chronicles of Narnia. The second book in that series, *Prince Caspian,* is dedicated to Havard's daughter Mary Clare.

The Inklings met for about seventeen years. Attendance was by invitation only, and there was a fixed procedure for inviting and introducing new people. Warren Lewis writes, "Someone would suggest that Jones be asked to come in of a Thursday, and there could be either general agreement, or else a perceptible lack of enthusiasm and a dropping of the matter."

Any violation of this rule resulted in open hostility. Those who came to meetings uninvited were called "gatecrashers," those who brought unannounced visitors were severely criticized, and those who had the nerve to elect themselves members at their own initiative were considered completely out of line. On one occasion, Warren Lewis was outraged when Tolkien (called "Tollers") brought an unwelcome guest, explaining that he and his brother were "much concerned this evening by the gate crashing of B; Tollers, the ass, brought him here last Thursday, and he has apparently now elected himself an Inkling. Not very clear what one can do about it."

Tolkien violated protocol more than once. Warren Lewis reports, "Tollers, to everyone's annoyance, brought a stranger with him, one [Gwyn] Jones, professor of English at Aberystwyth." This time, though, the stranger "turned out to be capital value." Warren records in his diary that "he read a Welsh tale of his own writing, a bawdy humorous thing told in a rich polished style which impressed me more than any new work I have come across for a long time."

Another evening did not end as happily. Here's the account: "Barfield made the mistake of presuming to bring a friend along unannounced— a serious *faux pas* that almost broke up the group when some members approved and others disapproved of the new candidate." Ultimately, the man was never invited back.

Charles Williams

One invited guest became a vital member of the group, though he arrived somewhat late on the scene. Charles Williams came to Oxford six years after meetings of the Inklings had begun. He was born and raised in London, and, in contrast to the other members, he strongly preferred life in the city. He worked as an editor at the London office of the Oxford University Press. Despite his demanding schedule as a senior editor, Williams was a prolific writer. He wrote seven books of poetry, four books of criticism, four of theology, seven biographies, seven novels, and dozens of plays, articles, and book reviews.

John Wain exclaims, "Williams! How many people have tried to describe this extraordinary man, and how his essence escapes them!"

Wain is right: Williams is very difficult to describe. A short piece published in 1947 calls him a "poet, mystic, scholar and novelist," and declares, "He was an astonishing and a very great figure to find in a world that for the most part lacked his double vision, and the seven novels are only a small part of what he left behind; writing of this kind will never be repeated, and the reading of his books is a disturbing experience which should not be missed."

Descriptions of Williams as intense, honest, fierce, disturbing, astonishing, and prophetic are repeated in one form or another by everyone who knew him. His coworker at the Press, Gerard Hopkins, emphasized the strength of Williams as a transforming presence who was able to change the ordinary everyday workplace by the "sheer force of love and enthusiasm." He had an unusual capacity for friendship; as Humphrey Carpenter explains, "At a first meeting he would talk as if he had known you for years, and as if it were the most natural thing in the world to discuss poetry or theology with you."

Williams's connection with the Inklings began with a serendipitous exchange of books. In 1935, Lewis completed *The Allegory of Love*, his first significant work of scholarship. He submitted the manuscript to Oxford University Press. Charles Williams read the proofs and was very impressed with it.

At the same time that Williams was preparing *The Allegory of Love* for publication, Lewis happened to be reading a copy of Williams's novel *The Place of the Lion*. Lewis loved the book and wrote a fan letter to Williams on 11 March 1936 to tell him so. He begins his letter somewhat hesitantly, then breaks into unabashed enthusiasm: "A book sometimes crosses ones path which is so like the sound of ones native language in a strange country that it feels almost uncivil not to wave some kind of flag in answer. I have just read your *Place of the Lion* and it is to me one of the major literary events of my life."

Lewis continues, listing four things about the book that he likes best: the pleasure of reading a good fantasy novel, the exploration of real philosophical and theological content, great characters, and "substantial edification." Lewis was impressed not only with these features, but also the skillful way that all of them were handled. He tells Williams, "Honestly, I didn't think there was anyone now alive in England who could do it."

Lewis concludes his letter with an invitation, offering both a warm welcome and a very fine description of the Inklings: "We have a sort of informal club called the Inklings: the qualifications (as they have informally evolved) are a tendency to write, and Christianity. Can you come down some day next term (preferably *not* Sat. or Sunday), spend the night as my guest in College, eat with us at a chop house, and talk with us till the small hours. Meantime, a thousand thanks."

Williams responded the next day, expressing his surprise: "If you had delayed writing another 24 hours our letters would have crossed. It has never before happened to me to be admiring an author of a book while he at the same time was admiring me." Then he muses that, somehow, God must be at the bottom of it: "My admiration for the staff work of the Omnipotence rises every day."

Lewis and Williams met about three months later, and they greatly enjoyed each other's company. They made it a point to get together several times a year. Lewis writes that his friendship with Williams "rapidly grew inward to the bone," and their friendship came to mean a great deal to both of them.

Lewis struggled to explain the effect that Williams had on others. He offered this description: "He is . . . of humble origin (there are still traces of cockney in his voice), ugly as a chimpanzee but so radiant (he emanates more *love* than any man I have ever known) that as soon as he begins talking . . . he is transfigured and looks like an angel." Lewis used this image more than once, adding this clarification: "not a feminine angel in the debased tradition of some religious art, but a masculine angel, a spirit burning with intelligence and charity."

In September of 1939, at the start of World War II, Oxford University Press moved its London offices to Oxford for safety. Williams moved with the Press, though his wife and son remained in London. As soon as he arrived, he became a regular, active member of the Inklings. Williams had a profound impact on the whole group, but he and Lewis enjoyed a particularly strong connection. Lewis describes him as "my great friend Charles Williams, my friend of friends, the comforter of all our little set, the most angelic." In the following tribute, Lewis captures the versatility and vigor of an Inklings meeting and the important part Charles Williams played:

[Williams's] face—angel's or monkey's—comes back to me most often seen through clouds of tobacco smoke and above a pint mug, distorted into helpless laughter at some innocently broad buffoonery or eagerly stretched forward in the cut and parry of prolonged, fierce, masculine argument and "the rigour of the game".

Such society, unless all its members happen to be of one trade, makes heavy demands on a man's versatility. And we were by no means of one trade. The talk might turn in almost any direction, and certainly skipped "from grave to gay, from lively to severe": but wherever it went, Williams was ready for it.

When the Inklings gathered, substantial intellect, enormous talent, and powerful personality met. And Williams was completely at home in the center of it all.

Ritual and Routine

As the group grew, the meeting time shifted from Monday mornings to Thursday evenings. But the defining activity remained the same. This was a group of working writers. They gathered in Lewis's rooms at Magdalen College, a setting described as "rather bleak":

The main sitting-room is large, and though certainly not dirty it is not particularly clean. . . . [Lewis] never bothers with ashtrays but flicks his cigarette ash . . . on to the carpet wherever he happens to be standing or sitting. He even absurdly maintains that ash is good for carpets. As for chairs—there are several shabbily comfortable armchairs and a big Chesterfield sofa in the middle of the room—their loose covers are never cleaned, nor has it ever occurred to Lewis that they ought to be. Consequently their present shade of grey may or may not bear some relation to their original colour.

Members would arrive sometime after dinner, usually around 9:00 p.m. According to Warren Lewis, "There was a tacit agreement that ten-thirty was as late as one could decently arrive." Meetings of the

Inklings followed a simple structure, and their opening ritual was always the same. When half a dozen members had arrived, Warren Lewis would produce a pot of very strong tea, the men would light their pipes, and C. S. Lewis would call out, "Well, has nobody got anything to read us?" Then "out would come a manuscript," and they would "settle down to sit in judgement upon it."

The range of texts read aloud at Inklings meetings was rich and remarkable. Tolkien read *The Lord of the Rings*. He also shared original poetry, a novel called *The Notion Club Papers,* and sections from *The Hobbit.* Williams read each chapter from *The Noises That Weren't There* and *All Hallows' Eve,* as well as his Arthurian poetry and an occasional play, including *Seed of Adam* and *Terror of Light.* Lewis read *Out of the Silent Planet, The Great Divorce, The Problem of Pain, Miracles,* and others, many of them chapter by chapter as they were written. He read many of his poems, and at one point, he shared a long section of his translation of Virgil's *Aeneid.* He also read *The Screwtape Letters* to the group, and according to Havard, "They really set us going. We were more or less rolling off our chairs."

Other members of the group attended less frequently and contributed less often. Nevill Coghill and Adam Fox read poetry, the former light lampoons and the latter more serious lyrics. David Cecil read *Two Quiet Lives,* a literary study of Dorothy Osborne and Thomas Gray. Colin Hardie read a paper on Virgil. Owen Barfield read fiction and a short play on Jason and Medea. John Wain read a number of his own poems and an essay on Arnold Bennett.

During the years the Inklings met, Warren Lewis began to write books about seventeenth- and eighteenth-century France, focusing on the reign of Louis XIV. His book *The Splendid Century* has become a standard text in its field. The Inklings observe that Warren Lewis often provided the best and most thought-provoking material read at Inklings meetings.

Listening to drafts and offering energetic feedback occupied the better part of every Inklings meeting. Warren Lewis makes it clear that the Inklings were unbiased in their judgments, observing, "We were no mutual admiration society." Havard adds, "Criticism was frank but friendly. Coming from a highly literate audience, it was often profuse and detailed."

There is nothing unusual about their procedure. Walter Hooper notes that this habit of reading papers aloud and submitting them for comment was typical of Oxford clubs. He writes, "The usual practice in most Oxford Societies—literary or otherwise—is for the speaker to *read a paper*. It is, I think I can safely say, as much the expected thing that a speaker will have a paper to read to his audience as that a student will have an essay in his hand when he goes to a tutorial."

Extensive reading, careful listening, and thoughtful critique marked these weekly meetings. Tolkien expressed heartfelt appreciation for the liveliness and candor of the group, noting even though the discussion often became heated, he felt safe from "contention, ill will, detraction, or accusations without evidence."

The Bird and Baby

One way to get a clearer picture of the Inklings is to contrast these Thursday meetings at Magdalen College with other, less formal gatherings that took place throughout the week. The Thursday writers group might be described as their center of gravity. It established their identity, defined their membership, and gave them their name. In a sense, the focus of the Inklings was quite specific.

And yet, the ongoing activity of the Inklings was flexible and wide-ranging. They met in small clusters of two or three to exchange manuscripts, give advice, or collaborate on various projects. They saw one another in many different venues: for lunch, dinner, or beer, or walking tours through the English countryside. They enjoyed a number of special celebrations. During wartime shortages, Lewis received occasional care packages from his American fans, and he would gather his friends and share needed supplies. There were special occasions, including a weekend celebration to mark the end of the war. Their literary influence flourished in many settings throughout the years they met.

Of these casual meetings, the best known was the gathering for lunch on Tuesdays. They met at an Oxford pub called The Eagle and Child, long referred to as "The Bird and Baby" by those who frequent it. These meetings were more open and public. Warren Lewis makes it clear they were separate from the Thursday writers group. He adds,

"Of course there was no reading on Tuesday." Tolkien's biographer, Humphrey Carpenter, agrees: "talking, rather than reading aloud, was the habit at these morning sessions in a pub."

Nathan Starr attended one of the Tuesday meetings. Recalling it years later, he, too, emphasizes its informality: "The conversation at The Bird and Baby was rather casual and general; I do not recall any sustained serious discussion." Unlike the Thursday meetings, this get-together at the pub can, indeed, be accurately described as just a gathering of friends, an assembly of those who had much in common and much to share.

In fact, Tuesday meetings at The Eagle and Child developed a reputation for being quite boisterous, partly as a result of Lewis's exuberance, partly the equally dynamic presence of men like Hugo Dyson and Nevill Coghill. One of the lesser-known members of the Inklings, James Dundas-Grant, emphasizes the drama and energy: "We sat in a small back room with a fine coal fire in winter. Back and forth the conversation would flow. Latin tags flying around. Homer quoted in the original to make a point." Even Professor Tolkien, often pictured as reserved and reflective, joined in the fray by "jumping up and down, declaiming in Anglo-Saxon." Lewis wondered what other people made of it all, suggesting "the fun is often so fast and furious that the company probably thinks we're talking bawdy when in fact we're v. likely talking Theology."

Famous and Heroic

Although there are plenty of controversies and disagreements about the Inklings, their energy, intellectual rigor, and creative intensity are never in doubt. And the Inklings are frank in expressing their appreciation for the group. Warren Lewis calls them "a famous and heroic gathering." He describes the talk, particularly his brother's, as "an outpouring of wit, nonsense, whimsy, dialectical swordplay, and pungent judgement such as I have rarely heard equalled." Havard echoes this sentiment, observing, "The talk was good, witty, learned, high-hearted, and very stimulating." John Wain, generally quick to carp and criticize, says of the Thursday meetings, "The best of them were as good as anything I shall live to see."

Lewis agreed. He asks, "Is any pleasure on earth as great as a circle of Christian friends by a good fire?" He emphasizes not only the thrill of the group, but also their significance: "What I owe to them all is incalculable."

Tolkien expressed his appreciation with characteristic artistry and enthusiasm, writing in imitation of his beloved *Beowulf:* "*Hwæt! we Inclinga, on ærdagum searopancolra snyttru gehierdon.*" Carpenter provides this translation: "Lo! we have heard in old days of the wisdom of the cunning-minded Inklings." The translation continues, "how those wise ones sat together in their deliberations, skillfully reciting learning and song-craft, earnestly meditating. That was true joy!"

DOING WHAT THEY DID: Great groups often grow from small beginnings. Lewis observes, "What we now call 'the Romantic Movement' once *was* Mr. Wordsworth and Mr. Coleridge talking incessantly (at least Mr. Coleridge was) about a secret vision of their own." Members meet often, and typically their surroundings aren't formal or fancy—the corner pub, a coffee shop, or a shabby sitting room will do. There are informal and spontaneous get-togethers as well as scheduled ones. And regularly scheduled meetings work best when there are predictable structures, almost as if the rhythm of routine creates a safe place to discuss daring possibilities.

Charles Williams at Oxford

CHAPTER THREE

The Heart of the Company

The Inklings have been called the 20th century's most influ-ential group of writers. But no matter how accomplished writers become, they still struggle with discouragement. Charles Williams knew this well. When his novel *All Hal-lows' Eve* was released, he waited anxiously for the public response. He wrote a letter to his wife, admitting, "The novel really gnaws me. I feel as if everyone would sneer at it. This is silly, because you liked a lot of it, and [T. S. Eliot] liked it, but there it is! You must forgive me and be kind."

Then, after two weeks of anxious waiting, Williams opened the *Daily Herald* and found this enthusiastic review: "A book by Charles Williams is an event. He is considered by some people our greatest liv-ing writer. I do not think he will ever be a popular writer, yet I venture to say that his work will go on when you and I and the book of that title have *Gone with the Wind*."

Williams was greatly encouraged. He forwarded a copy of the re-view to his wife and attached a short note. "It could hardly be better," he said. "All my love, & thank you for supporting *A. H. E.*"

Like Williams, C. S. Lewis also struggled with discouragement. Af-ter reading the proofs of his poem *Dymer*, he agonized, "I never liked it less. I felt that no mortal could get any notion of what the devil it was all about." He expressed similar doubts early in the writing of

Perelandra, telling his friend Sister Penelope, "I may have embarked on the impossible." And again, after working for more than ten years on *English Literature in the Sixteenth Century excluding Drama,* Lewis confided his fears to an American correspondent: "The book really begins to look as if it might be finished in 1952 and I am, between ourselves, pleased with the manner of it—but afraid of hidden errors."

As these examples from Williams and Lewis illustrate, the writing life can be an emotional roller-coaster ride. The excitement of creating is followed by desperate self-doubt. Courage and inspiration compete with discouragement and despair. For innovators in general and for writers in particular, one of the most valuable resources in the midst of these challenges is the presence of resonators.

What is a "resonator"? The term describes anyone who acts as a friendly, interested, supportive audience. Resonators fill many roles: they show interest, give feedback, express praise, offer encouragement, contribute practical help, and promote the work to others. The presence of resonators is one of the most important factors that marks the difference between successful writers and unsuccessful ones.

Resonators show interest in the work itself—they are enthusiastic about the project, they believe it is worth doing, and they are eager to see it brought to completion. But more importantly, they show interest in the writer—they express confidence in the writer's talents and show faith in his or her ability to succeed. They understand what the writer is attempting. They catch the vision and then do all they can. Resonators help innovators to make the leap from where they are to where they need to be.

Resonators are encouragers. Tolkien recognized this essential gift, expressing thanks to C. S. Lewis: "He was for long my only audience. Only from him did I ever get the idea that my 'stuff' could be more than a private hobby. But for his interest and unceasing eagerness for more I should never have brought [*The Lord of the Rings*] to a conclusion." Tolkien uses absolute terms when he describes Lewis's important role as a resonator. He says Lewis was his *only* audience. Lewis was the *only* one who encouraged him to seek a wider audience. Without him, Tolkien asserts, the book would *never* have been written.

In expressing his gratitude to Lewis, Tolkien does more than underscore the importance of resonators. He also suggests several of their most important actions. Resonators serve as an interested audience. They help move the text from the private sphere to the public sphere. As they eagerly anticipate new chapters, resonators inspire—or compel—the writer to produce new text in response. They pressure, push, and persuade the writer to bring long-term projects to a conclusion. And their enthusiasm for what has been done in the past may be just what it takes to encourage the writer to tackle brand-new projects.

Praise for Good Work

Resonators offer their support in a number of different ways, and the most obvious one is praise. Lewis firmly believed praise should be part of daily life. He asserts, "The world rings with praise—lovers praising their mistresses, readers their favourite poet, walkers praising the countryside, players praising their favourite game—praise of weather, wines, dishes, actors, motors, horses, colleges, countries, historical personages, children, flowers, mountains, rare stamps, rare beetles, even sometimes politicians or scholars."

For Lewis, praise is not only a natural part of life, but also one of the most important traits of a healthy mind. He observes, "The humblest, and at the same time most balanced and capacious, minds praised most, while the cranks, misfits and malcontents praised least." He sums it up this way: "Praise almost seems to be inner health made audible."

In many ways, the Inklings cultivated this habit of seeking what is good. Warren Lewis tells us that when the Inklings got together, "Praise for good work was unstinted." His response to *The Lord of the Rings* (called "the new Hobbit") illustrates this; it was generous, and it continued off and on for many years. In the following diary entries, Warren Lewis uses familiar nicknames: "Tollers" for Tolkien and "J" (short for Jack) for his brother.

10 October 1946 Tollers continued to read his new Hobbit: so *sui generis*, so alive with the peculiar charm of his "magical" writing, that it is indescribable—and merely worth recording here for an odd proof of how near he is to real magic.

24 *October 1946* Tollers read us a couple of exquisite chapters from the "new Hobbit." Nothing has come my way for a long time which has given me such enjoyment and excitement; as J says, it is more than good, it is great.

4 *July 1947* After dinner I read about half of the batch of [the new] Hobbit which Tollers sent me: how does he keep it up? The crossing of the marshes by Frodo, Sam and Gollum in particular is magnificent.

Praise for stories, poems, plays, lectures, articles, and essays is sprinkled throughout the letters and diaries of the Inklings. Writing to Charles Williams, Lewis characteristically begins with lavish praise: "Though I have not yet finished it I feel I must write and congratulate you on producing a really great book in your *He Came Down from Heaven.* It is thickly inlaid with patins of bright gold." Lewis continues, not merely offering general feedback, but investing significant energy to offer praise in detail. He congratulates Williams for "every word on p. 25." He praises one sentence in particular, exclaiming, "This is really overwhelming. I honestly think it quite likely that when we are in our graves this may become one of the sentences that straddle across ages like the great dicta of Plato, Augustine, or Pascal." Then there is a clever backhanded compliment: "And it's so *clear,* which at one time I should never have expected a book of yours to be."

And here is the sentence, written by Williams, the one Lewis called timeless and unexpectedly clear: "If, *per impossibile,* it could be divinely certain that the historical events upon which Christendom reposes had not yet happened, all that could be said would be that they had not *yet* happened."

Among the Inklings, praise was lavishly expressed and gratefully received. Williams clearly appreciated Lewis's enthusiasm—he comments in his letters that Lewis is the one person who really understands him. He writes to his wife, "Lewis says that my last Monday's address [a lecture on Milton] was 'the most important thing that has happened in the Divinity Schools for a hundred years, or is likely to happen for the next hundred.'"

It may seem that Williams is exaggerating Lewis's response, but Lewis's account of the same event suggests that he is not. Lewis shows his appreciation by describing the effect of this lecture on the students: "It was a beautiful sight to see a whole room full of modern young men and women sitting in that absolute silence which can *not* be faked, very puzzled, but spell-bound." In an echo of Williams's own account of the event, Lewis continues, "It was 'borne in upon me' that that beautiful carved room had probably not witnessed anything so important since some of the great medieval or Reformation lectures." He concludes, "I have at last, if only for once, seen a university doing what it was founded to do: teaching Wisdom."

C. S. Lewis writes movingly about Williams on a number of occasions, but he was by no means his only fan. Warren Lewis greatly appreciated him, writing the following letter to him in September of 1937, quite early in their friendship:

> This letter, though emanating from the above seat of learning [Oxford], is not from Lewis the English Tutor, but from his fat brother,—whom you may remember to have met on a couple of pleasant occasions, and who is glad to hear that there is a prospect of seeing you down here some time this term.
>
> I wanted to tell you how much I have enjoyed "Descent into Hell": though on second thoughts perhaps "enjoyed" is hardly the right word: I should rather say how much I appreciated it. Up to this I have always thought that the death of Sir Giles Tumulty [in *Many Dimensions*] was your high water mark, but the Descent seems to me far in a way better—it will be a long time before I forget those footsteps pattering through Battle Hill at night!!

This gracious and appreciative letter continues with more compliments, balanced with gentle criticism: "The only character whom I thought did not perhaps altogether pull his weight was the playwright: I don't quite know why, but he did not seem to me strong enough. All the rest I thought magnificent."

Other Inklings also wrote letters in praise of one another. C. S. Lewis and Nevill Coghill read one another's poetry and provided detailed feedback. Encouragement played a significant part in their exchange. When Coghill wrote a particularly enthusiastic response to *Dymer*, Lewis expressed his gratitude. "My dear Coghill," he writes, "It is as if you had given me a bottle of champagne—a dangerous moment and difficult to reply to."

Lewis and Barfield, friends since their days as undergraduates, regularly exchanged manuscripts and critiques, and many of these letters include high praise. In 1930, for example, Barfield sent Lewis an essay, along with a letter expressing doubts about the work and asking specifically for some honest feedback. Lewis reassured him, "Don't think it has failed either *per se* or in its effect on me. It is bathed in a golden cloud & drips with honey—well worth doing a good bit more on."

Such encouragement is typical of Lewis's feedback, which at times is downright extravagant. For example, when Barfield sent him a draft of his poem "The Tower," Lewis declared, "I have no doubt at all that you are engaged in writing one of the really great poems of the world." In a diary entry, Lewis praised this poem again, saying it is "full of magnificent material and never a dead phrase: the new part strong and savage."

Barfield himself confirms that Lewis thought highly of his work: "When [Lewis] read *Saving the Appearances,* he called it a 'stunner'; *Worlds Apart,* when it first came out, he said he found so exciting that he was in danger of reading it too quickly; and shortly before his death, when he was confined to his bed, he wrote to me that the two things that consoled him most were reading that book, *Worlds Apart,* and the *Iliad.*" Barfield was understandably pleased to see his novel mentioned side-by-side with Homer's *Iliad,* one of the enduring classics of western literature.

Not all of their feedback was this detailed or extensive. When Lewis finished writing a poem called "The Birth of Language," he sent it off to Barfield with a request for feedback, as was his custom. Barfield writes, "I have a very vivid memory of receiving it by post. I was very busy at the time and quite immersed in a non-literary milieu. I seized a postcard, wrote the one word 'Whew!' on it and dropped it in the letter box!"

Even though Tolkien was known to grumble, he, too, could be enthusiastic and generous in his praise of the work of his friends. When Lewis had trouble finding a publisher for *Out of the Silent Planet*, Tolkien wrote two letters to Stanley Unwin, urging him to publish it. Tolkien not only expresses his admiration for the work, but also bolsters his opinion by invoking the consensus of the Inklings. He writes, "I read it, of course; and I have since heard it pass a rather different test: that of being read aloud to our local club (which goes in for reading things short and long aloud). It proved an exciting serial, and was highly approved." Tolkien praises the novel's language, its poetry, its inventiveness, and its "spice of satire." With flourish, he concludes, "I at any rate should have bought this story at almost any price if I had found it in print, and loudly recommended it."

He liked *Out of the Silent Planet;* he also liked the second book in the series, *Perelandra,* calling it "a great work of literature." And when he read the third book, *That Hideous Strength,* he explained that even though he didn't consider it a "proper conclusion" to Lewis's Ransom Trilogy, it was certainly "good in itself." Others have echoed this view.

Tolkien wrote a long description of Lewis's "Myth Became Fact," praising it highly and calling it "a most interesting essay." He was enthusiastic about *Letters to an American Lady,* saying he found it "deeply interesting and very moving." And he called *English Literature in the Sixteenth Century* "a great book."

Taken all together, Tolkien's response to C. S. Lewis's works was somewhat mixed, as we will see in the next chapter. But he had nothing but praise for the writing of Warren Lewis. Tolkien admitted that he was not inherently interested in the historical subjects Warren Lewis explored. Even so, he was captivated by the skill and grace of the writing itself, calling it witty and learned, "very good," and "very amusing."

All of the Inklings encouraged one another, but Charles Williams seems to have been uniquely gifted at it. Williams's biographer, Alice Mary Hadfield, explains that Williams had this effect on everyone he met, whether a stranger at a bus stop or an old, familiar friend. She summarizes his impact as follows: "C. W. could make each one seem important and interesting, a vital gift to most of us, but even more than that, he could make life important and interesting, not some life removed from us by money, opportunity or gifts, but the very life we had to lead and should probably go on leading for years."

W. H. Auden highlights this when he says, "In his company one felt twice as intelligent and infinitely nicer than, out of it, one knew oneself to be."

Williams brought a unique quality to the Inklings, to the classroom, to personal relationships, and to his workplace. What was the exact nature of this transforming presence? Gerard Hopkins puts it this way: "He found the gold in all of us and made it shine." Although all of the Inklings were quick to praise, Williams charged the very atmosphere with praise and encouragement wherever he went.

Pressure and Perseverance

Generally, resonators provide encouragement in a positive, nurturing way. But there is another form of encouragement, one that is forceful, even coercive, in nature. There is a hint of this in the interaction between Lewis and Tolkien. Tolkien explains that when he produced text that was not up to par, Lewis would turn to him and say, "You can do better than that. Better, Tolkien, please!" Tolkien writes, "I would try. I'd sit down and write the section over and over." Lewis admits that his part in Tolkien's writing process often "carried to the point of *nagging*."

In fact, when a reader wrote to Lewis to ask if Tolkien was working on another book, Lewis confessed, "When you'll get any more in print from him, Lord knows. You see, he is both a procrastinator & a perfectionist."

Tolkien needed the pressure. He required the presence of others in order to keep writing, and his work on *The Hobbit* is a good example. Tolkien drafted most of it in 1930 and 1931. He read it to his sons and showed it to C. S. Lewis, who had a "delightful time" reading it and declared that, apart from the rough ending, he thought it was "really *good*." In the summer of 1936, some staff members at Allen & Unwin Publishing Company learned of the story and urged Tolkien to finish it. Responding to their interest, he completed the book and submitted it on 3 October 1936. It was published about a year later. A word of praise, a publisher, and a looming deadline were the ingredients Tolkien needed in order to bring that project to a close.

Pressure continued to play an important role in Tolkien's writing process. Responding to his publisher once more, Tolkien recorded cautiously on 19 December 1937, "I have written the first chapter of a new story about Hobbits." He struggled to make progress, and as he wrote, the book took on a life of its own, gaining darker elements and becoming much more layered and complex. But by August 1938, Tolkien reported that the book was "getting quite out of hand." The project that had begun as just another Hobbit story—suitable for children and filled with picnics, parties, fireworks, riddles, and pranks—had become richer, more complicated, and much more challenging to write.

Tolkien was discouraged. By 1942, he was uncertain about the direction of the story, complaining that he "did not know how to go on." There were a number of factors weighing him down. For one thing, given the shortages and distractions of wartime, Tolkien had begun to wonder if the publication of such a long book was even a possibility.

Despite these deep misgivings, Tolkien told Unwin that he hoped to finish the book within the next few months. Instead, he abandoned it altogether, and "not a line on it was possible for a year."

Tolkien was *"dead stuck."* Then, on 29 March 1944, he had lunch with C. S. Lewis. Lewis provided encouragement in two different ways. First, he shared his own work in progress. Tolkien records, "The indefatigable man read me part of a new story!" In the act of sharing his own work, Lewis challenged Tolkien, providing more than a hint of friendly rivalry.

But Lewis also goaded him directly, urging him to get back to work and finish his book. Grumbling, yet appreciative, Tolkien writes, "He is putting the screw on me to finish mine. I needed some pressure, & shall probably respond."

This talk with Lewis proved to be a critical turning point. Five days after their meeting, on 3 April 1944, Tolkien writes, "I have begun to nibble at [*The Lord of the Rings*] again. I have started to do some (painful) work on the chapter which picks up the adventures of Frodo and Sam." And two days after that, Tolkien writes, "I have seriously embarked on an effort to finish my book, & have been sitting up rather late: a lot of re-reading and research required. And it is a painful sticky business getting into swing again." From that time, Tolkien reports steady, significant progress and records that Lewis and the others offered frequent praise for the chapters he read at Inklings meetings.

Resonators made the difference. Tom Shippey asserts, "I am sure that Tolkien would never have finished *The Lord of the Rings* without Lewis continually encouraging him and urging him on." Carpenter says that Tolkien very nearly abandoned the whole project and confirms that his decision to press on was "chiefly due to the encouragement" of C. S. Lewis.

Did his encouragement make any difference? After all, Lewis famously declared "No-one ever influenced Tolkien—you might as well try to influence a bandersnatch." It is a bold statement. But is it true?

Ultimately, Tolkien himself provides the answer, making it clear that he appreciated his friends and more: he recognized that they were crucial to his writing process. He writes, "But for the encouragement of C. S. L. I do not think that I should ever have completed or offered for publication *The Lord of the Rings*." And again, "Only by his support and friendship did I ever struggle to the end of the labour." And again, "I owe to his encouragement the fact that in spite of obstacles (including the 1939 war!) I persevered and eventually finished *The Lord of the Rings*."

Lewis may have wondered from time to time if all his "nagging" made a difference. But the evidence is overwhelming; it made all the difference in the world.

The Wager

The rocky and uneven path that led to the completion of *The Hobbit* and *The Lord of the Rings* shows just how important encouragement and accountability can be. But what about the spark that inspires a project in the first place? What part do resonators play? Tolkien finished *The Lord of the Rings* in 1949, but the mutual influence of Tolkien and Lewis began many years before.

In 1936, Tolkien and Lewis were largely unknown and unpublished authors, even though they had been writing all of their lives. Then Lewis read *The Place of the Lion* by Charles Williams and *A Voyage to Arcturus* by David Lindsay. The two novels are very different from one another, but they share one important trait: they offer a skillful blend of popular fiction with spiritual ideas. Lewis found the combination compelling, but he was hard-pressed to find other books that succeeded in quite the same way.

With this in mind, he approached Tolkien with a proposal: "Tollers, there is too little of what we really like in stories. I am afraid we shall have to try and write some ourselves." The two men talked a while and then tossed a coin, deciding Lewis would write about space travel and Tolkien would write about time travel. Tolkien elaborates, "We originally meant each to write an excursionary 'Thriller'; a Space-journey and a Time-journey (mine) each discovering Myth."

Lewis went home and started *Out of the Silent Planet.* It appears that as he began writing, his wager with Tolkien was heavy on his mind. His main character, Elwin Ransom, is a professor and an expert in languages. His name, "Elwin," means "Elf-friend."

Out of the Silent Planet was finished in September 1937 and published one year later, followed by *Perelandra* (1943) and *That Hideous Strength* (1945).

Tolkien's effort to write time-travel, which he called "The Lost Road," was never completed. Tolkien explains, "My effort, after a few promising chapters, ran dry: it was too long a way round to what I really wanted to make, a new version of the Atlantis legend." The fragment and Christopher Tolkien's illuminating commentary on it have been published in *The Lost Road and Other Writings.*

Although Tolkien did not make much progress with "The Lost Road," the wager that inspired it still proved fruitful. "The Lost Road" is intimately connected with another project called "The Fall of Númenor." In fact, it is not only the basis for that work, but also for the whole concept behind it. Christopher Tolkien has concluded that Númenor as a distinct part of Tolkien's mythology "arose in the actual context of his discussions with C. S. Lewis."

There is more. Tolkien suggests that *The Lord of the Rings* itself was the result of this single conversation, this famous wager. Reflecting back to the wager as his starting point, he writes, "At last my slower and more meticulous (as well as more indolent and less organized) machine has produced its effort. The labour! I have typed myself nearly all of it *twice*, and parts more often; not to mention the written stages!" Tolkien concludes, "But I am amply rewarded and encouraged to find that the labour was not wasted."

Out of the Silent Planet, Perelandra, That Hideous Strength, "The Lost Road," "The Fall of Númenor," *The Lord of the Rings.* Each one has a long and intricate history. But they all have their genesis in the same place. They were born out of a specific conversation, a friendly competition, the toss of a coin, and a challenge to write thrillers, each one "discovering Myth."

"Think of a Subject"

We tend to think of writers creating their work from deep wells of personal inspiration. But often a creative spark is struck from some kind of external circumstance. The Inklings received ideas and motivation from a number of outside sources—Tolkien's publisher asking for another Hobbit book, for example, or Lewis's publisher asking him to write something on the problem of pain, or the wager between Tolkien and Lewis.

Charles Williams regularly sought suggestions for new projects. On 21 June 1940, as he wrapped up several writing projects, he sent an urgent letter to his wife: "Think of a subject for a new novel, I beg you; let it be supernatural this time, because I am more certain there." Her suggestions helped shape the direction of his next novel, which opens with a discussion between two dead women as they walk the streets of London.

Owen Barfield also responded to ideas and suggestions from others. Barfield explains: "I had casually remarked to my friend C. S. Lewis that I seemed to be feeling an impulse to write a play in verse and was wondering about a subject . . . I recall the occasion very clearly and, though I am not reproducing his exact words, he said in effect: 'Why not take one of the myths and simply do your best with it—Orpheus for instance?' To which my mental reaction was, after some reflection: Well, why not?"

The mood of this conversation is comfortable and low key: Barfield asks for an idea, Lewis throws out a very specific suggestion, Barfield says, "Well, why not?" and then he gets to work. Both the ease and the specificity are typical of the interactions of these two Inklings and quite characteristic of the way the group worked. When Barfield produced *Orpheus*, Lewis was thrilled with the result. The play influenced him deeply, and he confessed, "Act II is simply superb. It brought tears to my eyes."

Like Williams and Barfield, Lewis was open to ideas for new projects. One came from Inkling James Dundas-Grant. Lewis was ill, and Dundas-Grant went to visit him in an Oxford nursing home. He recalls, "I leaned over the end of the bed and watched him, obviously under drugs. One eye opened. 'Hullo, D. G. Nice to see you.' He drowsed off again, and as I was about to slip out I heard him say, 'Not going yet, are you?' and he stirred up fully awake. After a brief chat, I said, 'Jack, I wish you'd write us a book about prayer.' 'I might', he said, with a twinkle. Then he dozed off again."

Lewis's last book was *Letters to Malcolm, Chiefly on Prayer*.

"It's Catching!"

Warren Lewis, one of the most active and talented members of the Inklings, benefited a great deal from the group. He became a published writer as the direct result of their example. Warren had worked on different writing projects throughout his life. As a child, he wrote imaginative tales of India, and as an adult, he kept a diary that shows his talent for graceful prose.

His first extended writing project was to compile and edit his family papers. He describes the work as follows:

My father died in 1929 . . . and when we came to examine his papers we found that he had never destroyed *anything*—not even the stubs of his used cheque books. All this material was shipped over to my brother's rooms in Magdalen College, Oxford, and we decided vaguely to sort it out at some future date. I retired in 1931 and came to live in Oxford myself. I had not begun to write in those days and wanted some occupation, so I went through this mass of documents, and decided—more or less as a joke—that I should compile and type

'The Lewis Papers'. This I did, including diaries in addition to letters, and covering a period 1850–1930.

Warren Lewis spent more than four years selecting, typing, and arranging these materials. He ended up with eleven volumes of *The Lewis Papers*. When they arrived from the binders, he pronounced the project a great success and declared that he was delighted with it. These volumes are a monumental achievement, offering a compelling account of the time. They are available to scholars at The Wade Center, Wheaton College, and they remain one of the most important sources of information we have about Lewis and his friends and family.

Despite the success of this project, it was not until some time later that Warren Lewis thought of writing anything for publication. He had a keen interest in the past and had been reading and writing about French history for many years. In 1934, he started to work with the material more deliberately, but he saw little value in the exercise. He notes in his diary, "I now write from time to time, a doggerel history of the reign of Louis XIV, to my own intense amusement, and, being under no illusions as to its practical value, do not see any danger in so doing." Like Tolkien, he never imagined that his writing would amount to anything more than a private hobby.

What inspired this retired army officer to take his writing more seriously? He was encouraged by the example of the Inklings. On 13 April 1944, Tolkien sent a report of an Inklings meeting in a letter to his son Christopher. Warnie is writing a book, he says, then adds with apparent pride, "It's catching!" Tolkien was more than enthusiastic—he calls Major Lewis's book the best entertainment of the evening. This literary dabbler found the atmosphere of the Inklings contagious. Warren Lewis became an active, accomplished author due to the modeling of the group.

Warren Lewis published seven books on seventeenth-century France, all highly praised. One of these, *The Sunset of the Splendid Century*, earned this accolade: "This book has not only scholarship; it has wit and a warm insight into human nature—endowments which are not always found in an historian." Another reviewer claimed that his "readability, wit and good sense almost equalled his brother's work."

The Inklings made a significant difference. Late in his life, Warren Lewis observed that his earnings as an author came to a total of £9,766 10d. He records with some wonder, "Not so bad for a complete amateur who was over fifty eight when he turned author!" He tells us that his brother had urged him to try his hand at writing earlier. But as it turned out, his career as an author was to flourish later, within the context of a supportive and active group.

Anticipation

There is another way that sharing your work in a group can shape a piece of writing. It is more subtle and harder to trace. But it may be just as profound as the influence of praise, pressure, competition, or example. Most writers find it easier to write when they have specific deadlines. When they meet in a group, each meeting provides accountability. Week after week, the Inklings knew they would face the same question: "Well, has nobody got anything to read us?" This motivated them to stay on track and make regular progress on their manuscripts.

Also, when writers are part of a group that meets at regularly scheduled times, they may begin to write with that particular audience in mind. They work deliberately to attract certain kinds of compliments. They revise in order to avoid particular kinds of criticism. It certainly seems likely that as C. S. Lewis sat at his writing desk, his thoughts might have run something like this: "If I use this phrase, it might offend Charles. I'd better define this term, or Owen will have something to say about it. That description is awkward; Tolkien won't like it. I'd better take some time, think it over, and rewrite it."

The Inklings adjusted what they said and how they said it in anticipation of the questions, concerns, biases, and tastes of this ever-present audience. Owen Barfield admits to just this kind of anticipation. He says, "If I'm writing anything to do with the theory of knowledge, with the nature of thought, I find myself always putting it in the form of a question to myself: Is this something that Jack could knock down? Is it something which is proof against any objection he would raise?"

Was this kind of anticipation also important to Tolkien? It looks that way. One indication may be the distinct difference between two of his books: *The Silmarillion* and *The Lord of the Rings*.

The Silmarillion did not develop in the context of an eager audience. Tolkien wrote it for his own amusement, for he found the myths and genealogies and languages of Middle-earth endlessly fascinating.

The Lord of the Rings, in contrast, was written to satisfy the demands of a publisher; Tolkien began "the new Hobbit" unwillingly. And he read it aloud, chapter by chapter, as it was written. It was critiqued and revised in a circle of interested readers.

Tolkien was completely aware of the difference in these two projects. He writes, "*The Silmarillion* is quite different [from *The Lord of the Rings*], and if good at all, good in quite another way." *The Silmarillion* contains some of the most beautiful passages Tolkien has ever written, but it is demanding to read, challenging to connect with, and far less popular. Author Gareth Knight characterizes the influence of the Inklings this way: "Tolkien began to come out of his Silmarillion shell and opened up gradual access to that world, first with *The Hobbit*, and then, like the slow opening of a flower, *The Lord of the Rings*."

There is something of a parallel between Tolkien's *The Silmarillion* and Lewis's *The Pilgrim's Regress:* both are among their authors' least accessible texts, and both were written apart from the Inklings. Lewis himself recognized the difficulty of his book. In a letter to a reader, Lewis says, "I don't wonder that you got fogged in *Pilgrim's Regress*. It was my first religious book and I didn't then know how to make things easy. I was not even trying to very much." We can credit the Inklings for serving as a lively, interested audience. They helped both Tolkien and Lewis learn how to write for general readers in the many books that followed.

A Cup of Tea

The role of a resonator is capacious and powerful, and yet, very often it is lived out in small and rather ordinary ways: paying bills, running errands, providing meals, buying books, handling mundane chores, typing or retyping texts, and sharing research materials or study space.

During the time that Charles Williams lived in Oxford, both his living space and workspace were severely cramped. He shared a large house at 9 South Parks Road, close to the center of Oxford. The bedrooms were not heated, so in the evenings, the members of the household gathered around the fire in the sitting room. It was a congenial group, but the lack of privacy made it difficult for a writer. Williams sat among them, writing poems, plays, and stories on a little pad of paper that he rested on his knee.

If his living situation was distracting and uncomfortable, his office space was worse: his employer had created space for him in an unused bathroom. Apparently, he made the best of it: "It was a large roomy bathroom, leading off the first-floor landing and overlooking the entrance. The covered bath made a good shelf for piles of manuscripts and books."

Sensitive to his friend's needs, C. S. Lewis encouraged Williams to use his rooms at Magdalen College as a more congenial place to work. Williams reports to his wife in a letter: "It is all very still. I have fled to Lewis's rooms; the College is silent all round me. I shall only go back to supper. He is [a] great tea-drinker at any hour of night or day, and left a tray for me with milk & tea, & an electric kettle at hand. Sound man! You must come here one day and see my refuge." It is clear that Williams appreciated Lewis's thoughtfulness. He was grateful for the practical assistance and the cheer of a good cup of tea.

Lewis's rooms at Magdalen served as a refuge for Warren Lewis as well. Their house, the Kilns, was a lively household, consisting of the Lewis brothers, Janie Moore, her daughter Maureen, Fred Paxford the gardener, and a variety of cooks, housekeepers, and other help. They also kept a number of animals, including dogs and cats.

Warren Lewis described it as "a house which was hardly ever at peace for 24 hours, amid senseless wranglings, lyings, backbitings, follies, and *scares*." Consequently, he kept most of his books in his brother's rooms at Magdalen and spent his mornings there, researching and writing. One of Lewis's students, Helen Tyrrell Wheeler, had this experience when she came to visit: "My other tutors, Dame Helen Gardner and Lord David Cecil, lived in elegant, orderly eighteenth-century rooms which always seemed full of brightness: sunshine or firelight or both. Quite different was Lewis's. There were of course books everywhere, but that was true of every room one went into in Oxford. These books had *taken over*—so that comfort had long departed. It was quite a business to find seats."

From time to time during her tutorial, Wheeler would catch a glimpse of Warren Lewis at work. She remembers, "There would, now and again, appear a very stealthy figure, who with a murmured greeting would track down a wanted book and disappear again into limbo. This, we gathered, was Lewis's brother. Informed opinion in Oxford at the time held that he was the world's greatest authority on all those families of that French aristocracy who had suffered during the Revolution; and that he knew the tiniest detail of their disastrous lives. I have no idea if this interesting belief is correct." It was.

Fanfare

The Inklings lavished considerable time and talent on each other's work in progress. This may have been something as simple as purchasing copies of the work. We know, for example, that John Wain's first book, a slim collection of nineteen poems entitled *Mixed Feelings,* was printed in a limited edition of 120 numbered copies and six of the Inklings—Lewis, Tolkien, Havard, Dyson, Coghill, and Warren Lewis—are named on the list of "subscribers before publication."

They also shared books with one another. Nevill Coghill's decision to give Lewis his copy of Williams's novel *The Place of the Lion* is a typical act of promotion, and a powerful one, for it ultimately paved the way for Williams to join the Inklings.

Lewis lent Tolkien his copy of *The Silver Trumpet,* a fairy tale written by Barfield. Sometime later, Lewis wrote to Barfield to tell him of the enthusiastic reception: "It is the greatest success among [Tolkien's] children that they have ever known. His own fairy-tales, which are excellent, have now no market: and its first reading—children are so practical!— led to a universal wail 'You're not going to give it back to Mr. Lewis, are you?'" The letter ends with this quick comment: "Cecil [Harwood] now has *The Place of the Lion:* get it out of him before he returns it to me."

Furthermore, the Inklings made it a habit to recommend books to others. For example, Williams tells his colleague Lois Lang-Sims, "You must read CSL's *Allegory of Love*—a great book on European poetry from Rome to Spenser: you might, I think, like it." Lewis tells a student that he should read *Sir Gawain and the Green Knight*, but makes it clear he must use the Tolkien/Gordon edition and no other. Lewis enjoins his friend Sister Penelope, "Do you know the works of Charles Williams? Rather wild, but full of love and excelling in the creation of convincing *good* characters."

They also wrote and published more than forty reviews in order to promote their work to the largest possible audience. Williams wrote many reviews, including two different endorsements of *The Screwtape Letters*. One was published in *The Dublin Review*. Williams explains that he wants to lend his voice to "reinforce the general recommendation" of Lewis's book. He adds that he not only admires its skill, but also finds it edifying: he recommends it "with the personal sincerity of one who has found himself warned and enlightened."

The other review was published in *Time & Tide*, and the whole review is written as an imitation of Screwtape himself, as if one devil is writing advice to another. Williams's review begins, "My dearest Scorpuscle." In the last paragraph he warns his readers that Lewis's book is "heavenly," and, therefore dangerous. He writes, "I hate it, this give-away of hell." Williams signs the review "Your sincere friend, Snigsozzle."

Williams shows a similar blend of humor and insight in his review of *The Problem of Pain*. He has high praise for Lewis's skill as a writer, noting that his style is "what style always is—goodness working on goodness, a lucid and sincere intellect at work on the facts of life or the great statements of other minds." Poking fun at his own tendency toward obscurity, Williams explains that he does not intend to offer the reader a paraphrase of the book: "Mr Lewis's prose is known, and those who know it would not thank me for translating it into mine."

Lewis reviewed *The Hobbit* twice, once in *The Times Literary Supplement*, and again in *The Times*. Lewis praises Tolkien as a sub-creator: "No common recipe for children's stories will give you creatures so rooted in their own soil and history as those of Professor Tolkien." He adds a comment that is part compliment, part encouragement, and perhaps just a little part gibe at his friend's thoroughness. He writes that Tolkien "obviously knows much more about them than he needs for this tale." These and other references to the background mythologies of the story testify to Lewis's familiarity with this larger body of work. They also show Lewis giving generous praise to Tolkien in the area where Lewis himself struggled, the development of a detailed and internally consistent sub-created world.

In this review, Lewis also reflects his own conviction about the nature of children's literature, that no book can be said to be good for children unless it is also good for adults: "This is a children's book only in the sense that the first of many readings can be undertaken in the nursery. . . . Only years later, at a tenth or a twentieth reading, will they begin to realise what deft scholarship and profound reflection have gone to make everything in it so ripe, so friendly, and in its own way so true."

He adds, "It may be years before we produce another author with such a nose for an elf." He ends by predicting, accurately enough, "*The Hobbit* may well prove a classic."

Lewis also published two enthusiastic reviews of *The Lord of the Rings*. His majestic endorsements have been quoted so often that they have become part of the fabric of Tolkien studies: "Here are beauties which pierce like swords or burn like cold iron; here is a book that will break your heart." Lewis is unabashed in his enthusiasm: here is a story, he calmly insists, that "will soon take its place among the indispensables." He admires the story's structure, its theology, geography, paleography, languages, and characters. He even praises the giving of names: "The names alone are a feast, whether redolent of quiet countryside (Michel Delving, South Farthing), tall and kingly (Boramir [sic], Faramir, Elendil), loathsome like Smeagol, who is also Gollum, or frowning in the evil strength of Barad Dur or Gorgoroth; yet best of all (Lothlorien, Gilthoniel, Galadriel) when they embody that piercing, high elvish beauty of which no other prose writer has captured so much."

Lewis also offers the definitive answer to those who condemn this book because it is fantasy. "'But why', (some ask), 'why, if you have a serious comment to make on the real life of men, must you do it by talk-ing about a phantasmagoric never-never land of your own?' Because, I take it, one of the main things the author wants to say is that the real life of men is of that mythical and heroic quality." He continues, "The value of the myth is that it takes all the things we know and restores to them the rich significance which has been hidden by 'the veil of familiarity.' The child enjoys his cold meat (otherwise dull to him) by pretending it is buffalo, just killed with his own bow and arrow. And the child is wise. The real meat comes back to him more savoury for having been dipped in a story."

In this review, Lewis's writing is at its best; his use of description, metaphor, and the felicitous phrase is simply as good as it gets. He writes, "But in the Tolkienian world you can hardly put your foot down anywhere from Esgaroth to Forlindon or between Ered Mithrin and Khand, without stirring the dust of history." Lewis shows more than mere enthusiasm for this work; he knows it intimately, understands it fully, loves it deeply, explicates it faithfully, defends it fervently. It has touched him bone-deep.

Lewis also wrote two reviews of Williams's *Taliessin through Logres;* one of them, published in *Theology,* is a full eight pages long. He begins by acknowledging that the work is very hard to read. Lewis accuses Williams of misusing the English language. And, singling out one pas-sage in particular, he admits "the obscurities are to me impenetrable." However, Lewis reassures us that, despite these problems, it is worth pressing on: "The poem has greatness enough to justify the intensive study it exacts." He praises the work chiefly for its "combination of jag-ged weight and soaring movement, its ability to narrate while remain-ing lyric, and (above all) its prevailing quality of glory—its blaze."

These reviews are a concrete form of practical support. Each one does two important things: encourages the author and increases public aware-ness of the work. Of all the reviews of the Inklings' books, one stands out among the rest. When he was 13 years old, Christopher Tolkien tried to do his part to boost his father's sales. He writes, "In December 1937, two months after publication, I wrote to Father Christmas and gave *The Hobbit* a vigorous puff, asking him if he knew of it, and proposing it to him as an idea for Christmas presents." In his letter, Christopher tells the history of the story, explaining that his father had written it "ages ago, and read it to John, Michael, and me in our winter 'reads' after tea in the evening."

And then he offers Father Christmas this final encouragement: "It is my favourite book."

DOING WHAT THEY DID: It is virtually impossible to sustain faith in creative work alone, especially when a project extends over a long period of time. Harold Lasswell coined the term "resonators" to describe what is needed: not just words of encouragement or praise, but a whole range of activities, everything from helping to find an idea for a new project to promoting the work to a much larger public.

When something resonates, it vibrates at the same frequency as something else—the wooden body of a violin, for example, catches and amplifies the sound that is made by the strings. Fundamentally, a resonator is someone who says, "I hear you. I understand what you are trying to do. I'll help you get there."

Owen Barfield on Addison's Walk

CHAPTER FOUR

"I've a good mind to punch your head."

All this talk about praise, encouragement, and mutual admiration is a bit misleading. While the Inklings were quick to praise one another, they were also highly critical. To use a phrase much loved by Lewis, the Inklings were "hungry for rational opposition." For what good is a creative group without critique, debate, and the clashing of perspectives? As Warren Lewis says, positive comments and negative ones are really two sides of the same coin: "Praise for good work was unstinted, but censure for bad work—or even not-so-good work—was often brutally frank." In fact, if there is anything that the Inklings express more often than gratitude for encouragement, it is healthy respect for conflict.

Havard expresses it best: Lewis "read *The Screwtape Letters* to us. And very hilarious evenings they were. And we enjoyed them very much. But he had no need to ask, 'What did we think of it?' We were all too ready to say what we thought of it. This was the ethos of the whole thing. That criticism was free."

Criticism was free, and it could be ferocious. Warren Lewis describes their conversations as "dialectical swordplay" and tells us, "To read to the Inklings was a formidable ordeal." The language of fighting and warfare is everywhere. Owen Barfield asserts, "You can't really argue keenly, eagerly, without being a bit aggressive." Barfield expresses his experience vividly. He says that in conversation with Lewis, he felt like he was "wielding a peashooter against a howitzer."

Lewis makes no excuses. He says an aggressive approach is something he learned in school, in what he calls "the rough academic arena." Lewis spent more than two years studying with William T. Kirkpatrick, a strict, logical, and demanding tutor known as the "Great Knock." This was undoubtedly one of the influences that shaped Lewis's appetite for intellectual swordplay.

Even praise and appreciation were sometimes expressed using rough, combative language. After reading *He Came Down from Heaven*, Lewis tells Williams, "You go on getting steadily better ever since you first crossed my path: how do you do it? I begin to suspect that we are living in the 'age of Williams' and our friendship with you will be our only passport to fame." Then Lewis adds, "I've a good mind to punch your head when we next meet."

When the Inklings describe their Thursday meetings, the overwhelming impression is that of great minds equaling and countering one another in grand intellectual battle. Tolkien, for example, describes what he calls a "great event" in November of 1944. Williams, Havard, Barfield, and Lewis were there. Lewis and Barfield launched into an argument, and Tolkien writes, "The result was a most amusing and highly contentious evening, on which (had an outsider eavesdropped) he would have thought it a meeting of fell enemies hurling deadly insults before drawing their guns."

At another meeting, an argument arose about the proper interpretation of Matthew 7:14, which reads, "Strait is the gate, and narrow is the way, which leadeth unto life, and few there be that find it." Lewis recalls the event this way: "I had a pleasant evening on Thursday with Williams, Tolkien, and Wrenn, during which Wrenn *almost* seriously expressed a strong wish to burn Williams, or at least maintained that conversation with Williams enabled him to understand how inquisitors had felt it right to burn people. Tolkien and I agreed afterwards that we *just* knew what he meant: that as some people . . . are eminently kickable, so Williams is eminently combustible."

It is an odd juxtaposition: in the context of a pleasant evening and agreeable conversation, which happens to be about the proper interpretation of scripture, the discussion gathers such intensity that Williams is deemed "combustible" by his close friends.

And that passage from the Bible? Lewis says that the group reached this conclusion: "Our Lord's replies are never straight answers and never gratify curiosity, and that whatever this one meant its purpose was certainly not statistical."

This scene was entirely typical. "Criticism was free," and it seems that of all the company, Charles Williams was most regularly and roundly criticized. In dismissing *Taliessin through Logres*, for example, Havard summarizes it as "a poem of epic dimensions, very Welsh and of an obscurity beyond belief." Elsewhere, he confesses "when it came to reading his work, I couldn't understand a word of it." Hugo Dyson, never one to mince words, scorned Williams's poetry as "clotted glory from Charles."

The Inklings were not the only ones who struggled with Williams's poems. Both W. H. Auden and T. S. Eliot liked Williams as a person and admired the work he did, but even they admit that reading Williams is a challenge. Auden writes, "I must confess that, when I first tried to read his poetry, though as a fellow verse writer I could see its great technical interest, I could not make head or tail of it." And after reading and rereading one of Williams's books in manuscript, T. S. Eliot wrote a letter to Williams urging him to revise the table of contents and the introduction and warning him that his complex imagery was so dense and difficult it would frighten the readers away.

When Williams sent Lewis some of his poetry, Lewis responded: "You will not be surprised to learn that I found your poems excessively *difficult*." He discusses several of them, offering praise, then continues to grumble about others that he "definitely disliked."

Lewis concludes this letter unequivocally: "I embrace the opportunity of establishing the precedent of brutal frankness, without which our acquaintance begun like this would easily be a mere butter bath!" The Inklings were committed to avoiding this "butter bath," and they were intentional in giving real, substantial critique. Once Barfield suggested that Lewis had been too soft on Williams; Lewis countered, "Don't imagine I didn't pitch into C. W. *for his obscurity* for all I was worth."

The Inklings, and others, accused Williams of being controversial, obscure, complex, and unnecessarily difficult. How did he respond? With gratitude. His views were stretched, his talents matured as he worked within this demanding context. He believed that all this feedback, harsh as it was, helped to keep him on track and improve his work. He expressed his appreciation succinctly, saying, "They are good for my mind."

But the most intense intellectual battle between Inklings didn't revolve around Charles Williams. It erupted between Lewis and Barfield, and it started much earlier, years before the Inklings got started.

The "Great War"

Combat was evident at regular Thursday meetings and again in more personal and informal settings. For example, on 26 January 1923, C. S. Lewis was just sitting down to dinner when he was surprised by a knock at his door. It was Owen Barfield. "The unexpected delight gave me one of the best moments I have had," Lewis writes. "We went at our talk *like a dogfight:* of Baker, of Harwood, of our mutual news."

Apparently, good-natured conflict erupted whenever Barfield and Lewis got together. Tolkien says that Barfield "tackled" Lewis, "making him define everything and interrupting his most dogmatic pronouncements." When Lewis summarized their relationship in *Surprised by Joy,* he characterized Barfield as "the man who disagrees with you about everything."

Over time, these intellectual skirmishes lengthened and deepened, becoming more formal and moving to the written page. For about nine years, roughly from 1922 to 1931, they sent letters back and forth, arguing about literature, language, poetry, and philosophy. Lewis describes the exchange as "an almost incessant disputation." They called it the "Great War."

These letters are not personal. They are really extended formal essays. Their tone is academic, and their language is extremely precise. Some are thickly illustrated with charts and diagrams, and many include numbered lists, articulating specific points of contention. This complex correspondence is full of references to literature, history, theology, and philosophy—both men constantly summarize, quote from, and refer to other thinkers and writers.

One thing stands out in these letters: their arguments were not conclusive. In fact, each one credits the other as having ultimately prevailed. Who won? That is hotly debated. What is unmistakable is this: the "Great War" made a powerful and lasting difference, but not because one of them convinced the other he was right. They listened and they learned. Both Barfield and Lewis clarified their own convictions. They modified their views. They expanded their understanding. Perhaps most importantly, they used these letters, year after year, to sharpen their skills. By exchanging arguments, listening, disagreeing, making adjustments and modifications, they learned how to ask and answer life's most serious philosophical questions. The impact of this great struggle was profound.

Lewis could not have developed as a religious apologist, novelist, or literary historian if he had not trained his intellect through these many years of extended arguments with his friend.

Barfield gained even more. He asserts that through these letters, Lewis taught him how to think.

His most important book, *Poetic Diction*, was forged in the context of this long debate. Once the book was completed, Lewis was the first person to read the manuscript. At Barfield's request, he responded with a long and detailed written analysis. These notes have been lost, so it is impossible to determine exactly how his comments impacted the final work. But we do know that Lewis thought chapter VII, "The Making of Meaning," was one of the "weakest portions" of the book. After Barfield read Lewis's comments, he responded by revising the book, then adding a new introduction and writing a whole new chapter to bolster the argument. Honest critique—pointing out shortcomings and suggesting new directions—helped this important book to be the best it could be.

In gratitude, *Poetic Diction* was dedicated to C. S. Lewis. And the dedication itself emphasizes the kind of influence he provided. Barfield thanks Lewis and then quotes William Blake, saying "Opposition is true friendship."

Something Better

The power of opposition is seen in other projects, including the changes Charles Williams made to one of his finest novels. The idea for a new book first came to him in May of 1943. He writes, "I now lie at night . . . with a kind of ghostly skeleton of a novel, and wake scared and unrefreshed."

He started working on it in mid-June, though he didn't have much of an idea for the plot. It is a detective story, set against the backdrop of war-torn London. In the opening scene, a young girl's body is discovered in an empty house. Neighbors believe the house is haunted, and a clairvoyant is brought in to investigate. Williams called this new novel *The Noises That Weren't There*.

Williams worked very hard on it and wrote three chapters. Then he read them to Lewis and Tolkien, and he shared them with his wife. All were unanimous in denouncing the draft, so Williams abandoned it. On the 3rd of September, he writes, "Three quarters of my mind is delighted that we are so at one about my discarded chapters; the other quarter is sad about the wasted work. Two months almost thrown away! But perhaps something better may come."

Hoping for the best, he started over. By the 23rd of September, he had made a new start, and soon he was making good progress. In a letter written on the 5th of October, he reports, "Waking at one . . . I got on with the novel, & wrote about a thousand words, going to sleep again about four. I hope to do some more this evening."

He called the new book *All Hallows' Eve*. It differs significantly from *The Noises That Weren't There,* but they share a number of important features. In both stories, the main character has supernatural abilities. Both include a character named Jonathan Drayton, a painter who is devoted to capturing the effects of light on canvas. And in both books, the plot revolves around a villain who creates human forms out of dust and water.

The key difference between the two novels lies in the way they are structured. *The Noises That Weren't There* is littered with extended explanations of hauntings and magic. *All Hallows' Eve* uses many of these same ideas, but instead of distracting from the tale, they are incorporated into the narrative and help carry the action forward. Overall, the pace of the story is dramatically improved.

As Williams wrote *All Hallows' Eve,* he read it to the Inklings, chapter by chapter, and he continued to revise it in response to their criticism. Many readers consider it one of Williams's best, and the Inklings played a significant role in it from start to finish. Tolkien notes, "I was in fact a sort of assistant mid-wife at the birth of *All Hallows' Eve,* read aloud to us as it was composed, but the very great changes made in it were I think mainly due to C. S. L." It is worth noting that Tolkien gives the group credit for bringing about "very great changes" and not just superficial adjustments. *All Hallows' Eve* was a deeply collaborative effort.

The Missing Chapter

The Noises That Weren't There is not the only example of a text that the Inklings rejected and the author abandoned. If you pick up a copy of *The Lord of the Rings* today, it ends with Sam saying, "Well, I'm back." But that is not where Tolkien ended his story. He wrote one more chapter, an epilogue. It was not an afterthought; it was not tacked on. It was part of his original vision. Christopher Tolkien emphasizes, "It is obvious from the manuscript that the text continued on without break."

This missing chapter opens about 15 years after Sam has returned from his difficult journey to Mordor and back. He has married Rosie Cotton and settled in Hobbiton with his family. "And one evening in March Master Samwise was taking his ease by a fire in his study, and the children were all gathered about him, as was not at all unusual, though it was always supposed to be a special treat."

Sam has been reading aloud from a large book on a stand, reading the tales written down in *The Red Book of Westmarch,* and talking about entwives and Lórien, Legolas, Gimli, Merry, Pippin, and Treebeard.

The children love these stories, and they seem to know them well. Sam's little son exclaims, "I want to hear about the Spider again. I like the parts best where you come in, dad." His daughter Elanor asks, "When can I go and see? I want to see Elves, dad, and I want to see my own flower."

Christopher Tolkien states with some emphasis, "It cannot be doubted that this was how he intended at that time that *The Lord of the Rings* should end." Here are the concluding paragraphs as they appear in the final draft of this last chapter:

> The stars were shining in a clear dark sky. It was the second day of the bright and cloudless spell that came every year to the Shire towards the end of March, and was every year welcomed and praised as something surprising for the season. All the children were now

in bed. It was late, but here and there lights were still glimmering in Hobbiton, and in houses dotted about the night-folded countryside.

Master Samwise stood at the door and looked away eastward. He drew Mistress Rose to him, and set his arm about her.

"March the twenty-fifth!" he said. "This day seventeen years ago, Rose wife, I didn't think I should ever see thee again. But I kept on hoping."

"I never hoped at all, Sam," she said, "not until that very day; and then suddenly I did. About noon it was, and I felt so glad that I began singing. And mother said: 'Quiet, lass! There's ruffians about.' And I said: 'Let them come! Their time will soon be over. Sam's coming back.' And you came."

"I did," said Sam. "To the most belovedest place in all the world. To my Rose and my garden."

They went in, and Sam shut the door. But even as he did so, he heard suddenly, deep and unstilled, the sigh and murmur of the Sea upon the shores of Middle-earth.

This epilogue has charmed the readers who have discovered it tucked away in the pages of *The History of Middle-earth*. However, when Tolkien finished rewriting and revising *The Lord of the Rings* and submitted it to his publisher, it did not contain an epilogue. Tolkien explains that he left it out because those he shared it with didn't like it. He writes, "An epilogue giving a further glimpse (though of a rather exceptional family) has been so universally condemned that I shall not insert it. One must stop somewhere." There is no specific record of who Tolkien is referring to here: his comment that the epilogue had been "universally condemned" may be a reference to several individual Inklings, or to the Inklings as a group, or to a larger circle that may have included his family and his publisher.

Against his better judgment, Tolkien agreed to drop the entire chapter. But he regretted this decision afterward. When the final volume of *The Lord of the Rings* was published, Tolkien protested: "I still feel the picture incomplete without something on Samwise and Elanor, but I could not devise anything that would not have destroyed the ending." It may be argued that instead of "destroying the ending," this missing chapter would have provided a sweet and satisfying close to the story. Tolkien thought so, but others disagreed, and so the epilogue, drafted and revised many times, has never been included in the published text.

"Brutally Frank"

All Hallows' Eve and *The Lord of the Rings* show that, for better or worse, criticism from the Inklings changed the books they were writing. However, much of the time, the impact of creative opposition is not so easily traced. Although the Inklings made many negative comments about one another's work, it can be hard to gauge the results of their comments. In his description of one Inklings meeting, for example, Warren Lewis reports that Colin Hardie "read an interminable paper on an unintelligible point about Virgil." Apparently, Warren Lewis wasn't the only one who disparaged this particular reading. John Wain remarked, "To say I didn't understand it is a gross understatement." In another instance, Warren Lewis attacks Barfield for issuing "withering discourse on the nothingness of the utterness."

Comments like these give us a record of how the members responded to particular works, and, taken together, they offer a snapshot of what meetings might have been like. Even when there is no record of how a particular comment may have changed a particular manuscript, these criticisms are likely to have stuck with the authors and changed the way they approached new projects. The same is true of criticism that appears in correspondence written after a book or article had already been published. Sometimes criticism impacts the work at hand; sometimes it changes the author.

Barfield gives this account of the process in a letter he wrote criticizing Lewis for redundancies in *Perelandra*:

> When his novel *Perelandra* appeared, I wrote [to Lewis] praising it highly but making one minor adverse criticism. There is a passage near the beginning of the book where Ransom, the returned space traveler, is endeavoring to describe his feelings about the Green Lady. In order to achieve this, the character in the book makes use of three

or four similes one after the other. I complained in my letter that I thought these held up the narrative and were more appropriate for an essay or lecture than a novel.

Lewis responded to Barfield's critique with ready agreement: "The devil of it is, you're largely right. Why can I never say anything *once?*" He continues, tongue in cheek, piling up illustrations of the very flaw he has just been accused of: "'Two and two make four. These pairs, in union, generate a quaternity, and the duplication of duplicates leaves us one short of five.' Well, all's one." Lewis continues in lighthearted self-mockery, using this same deliberate repetition in two other places in this letter. Clearly, he's gotten the message. His reply to Barfield is a classic Lewissian retort, both for its humor and for his willingness to accept criticism.

He concludes these playful comments with a quick jab aimed directly at Barfield: "And take that grin off your ugly face."

Lewis criticized Barfield's work in turn, challenging him not only about the work at hand, but also making more general observations about the habits of his writing style. In a letter written in 1962, Lewis critiques Barfield's new book, *Worlds Apart.* Characteristically, he starts out with lavish praise, emphasizing his enthusiasm for the work. He writes, "My trouble is that [it] is to me so exciting that I can't help reading it far too quickly. I must presently tackle it again and less greedily."

Then, without transition or any other fanfare, Lewis launches directly into criticism: "Your language sometimes disgruntles me. Why must it be *polyvalence* instead of *multivalence?*" He continues, criticizing a whole host of stylistic matters, pointing out recurring problems with sentence structure and clumsy word choice.

Other comments found in letters and diary entries further demonstrate that the Inklings did not like all that they found in one another's books. For example, when Warren Lewis read Lewis's *Problem of Pain,* he did not find the arguments compelling, nor the conclusion convincing. He writes, "I've never seen any explanation of the problem of pain (not even my brother's) which came near to answering the question for me."

If *The Problem of Pain* proved unsatisfying, there are other C. S. Lewis books that Warren Lewis found simply unreadable. He says that *Christian Reflections* was far above his head. And though he tried, he couldn't get very far through *Studies in Words.* He writes, "I've also (I'm afraid the only word is 'waded') half through J's *Studies in Words* but have had to abandon it—far too abstruse for me."

Tolkien also expresses dislike for quite a number of Lewis's books. However, in observing this, several cautions are in order. Tolkien describes himself as "a man of limited sympathies." Elsewhere, he says bluntly, "My taste is not normal." His preferences were specific, and his standards were high; in short, there are a lot of books by a lot of different authors that Tolkien did not particularly care for.

He takes serious issue with a number of points expressed in Lewis's book *Christian Behavior.* Tolkien challenges Lewis primarily on the basis of logical consistency—an area where Lewis is generally seen to be particularly strong—saying he finds a "confusion of thought" within the book itself.

Tolkien also didn't care for *The Great Divorce.* "I did not think so well of the concluding chapter of C. S. L.'s new moral allegory or 'vision,'" he writes. Tolkien never elaborates his reasons. It may be significant that he refers to it as a moral allegory, for he has said bluntly, "I dislike allegory wherever I smell it." Or it may be a reflection of his distaste for the use of a dream vision as a framing device, an important feature of the book's concluding chapter.

Tolkien criticized other Lewis books as well. Like Warren Lewis, he reacted strongly to *Studies in Words,* writing, "Alas! His ponderous silliness is becoming a fixed manner." He called *Letters to Malcolm* "a distressing and in parts horrifying work." He adds, "I began a commentary on it, but if finished it would not be publishable."

Tolkien's dislike for some of these books reflects his perspective on a much larger issue: his discomfort with Lewis's religious writings. Lewis scholar and historian Lyle W. Dorsett writes, "Lewis received much criticism for his preaching, teaching, and writing on Christian topics. Indeed, J. R. R. Tolkien was embarrassed that *The Screwtape Letters* were dedicated to him." The reason? Some felt that Lewis, "being neither a theologian nor an ordained clergyman, had no business communicating these subjects to the public."

Criticism of Lewis's work as a Christian apologist was widespread among academics at the time. Mary Rogers, a student at Oxford in the 1930s, explains that Lewis's lectures to those serving in the Royal Air

Force and his religious talks on the BBC were seen as a contribution to the war effort and, therefore, grudgingly accepted. However, "The publication of *The Problem of Pain* in 1940 raised academic eyebrows." And then Lewis really went too far: "When *The Screwtape Letters* were published in 1942, with his description as 'Fellow of Magdalen College, Oxford' on its title page, many of his colleagues were outraged. This was a best-seller. He was employed as a literary scholar, not a popular evangelist!"

Tolkien was well aware of this; in fact, he articulates it clearly and emphatically. In one letter, he takes note of "the extraordinary animosity that C. S. L. seems to excite in certain quarters." Elsewhere, he elaborates: "No Oxford don was forgiven for writing books outside his field of study—except for detective stories which dons, like everyone else, read when they are down with the 'flu. But it was considered unforgivable that Lewis wrote international best-sellers, and worse still that many were of a religious nature."

Lewis knew all of this, and it caused him much distress. He once told his friend Harry Blamires, "You don't know how I'm hated." His determination to defy academic protocol and openly express his Christian faith did more than alienate his friends and colleagues; it proved hazardous to his career. Lewis was passed over for promotion to two "coveted Chairs in English Literature at his university despite his scholarly claim to the appointments." It seems certain that his religious writing was the reason.

Clearly, the Inklings could be brutally frank in their critique of one another. Sometimes their words proved invaluable and transformed a work, and sometimes their words were ignored. And still other times, harsh words caused distress and harmed friendships. There is a balance to be met, and the Inklings sometimes failed to find it.

Denouncing Narnia

Though Tolkien attacked a number of Lewis's books, his strongest objections were aimed straight at The Chronicles of Narnia. There are a number of reasons for Tolkien's reaction, and they are rather complex.

It was February of 1949 when Lewis read the first three chapters of *The Lion, the Witch and the Wardrobe* to Tolkien. He was probably expecting an encouraging and helpful response. Instead, Tolkien said he thought the book was "about as bad as can be." Soon afterwards, Tolkien was talking with a friend about the story, and he erupted, "It really won't do, you know! I mean to say: *'Nymphs and their Ways, The Love-Life of a Faun.'* Doesn't he know what he's talking about?"

When Tolkien condemned the work, Lewis was taken aback. He thought highly of Tolkien's judgment, and he was astonished and hurt when Tolkien said that he thought the book was "almost worthless." Despite all his bluster, Lewis cared deeply about the opinions of others, and he relied a great deal on their encouragement. Throughout his letters, there are constant inquiries to friends, colleagues, and students asking whether or not a particular story or poem or other project is "any good" or if a rugged rough draft is "worth working on." If Lewis had considered Tolkien's response alone, Narnia might have been abandoned after two or three chapters.

But Lewis decided to give it one more try. On 10 March 1949, he had dinner with his friend and colleague Roger Lancelyn Green. Lewis read him the beginning of *The Lion, the Witch and the Wardrobe*. When he finished, he told Green that Tolkien had "disliked it intensely," and then asked, was it any good? Green told him the story was "more than good." Lewis, greatly encouraged, finished writing the whole novel by the end of the month. And then he continued the series, writing six more.

Tolkien disliked them all. For a long time, scholars and fans have debated why. Many different reasons have been offered.

Some say that Tolkien objected to the way Lewis haphazardly mixed together very different mythologies. David Graham explains, "To put Aslan, the fauns, the White Witch, Father Christmas, the nymphs, Mr. and Mrs. Beaver and the like—all of which had distinct mythological or imaginative origins—into a single imaginative country seemed like a terrible mistake." Another scholar, Joe R. Christopher, has argued that Tolkien was not concerned about the jumble of mythologies but their distortion. When Tolkien first expresses how much he hates the story, he specifically mentions Tumnus the Faun. Christopher speculates, "Tolkien is thinking in mythological terms—what is a faun? how can one be expected to act?" Tolkien understands that a faun, or satyr, is tradition-ally a sinister creature; however, in this story, Tumnus is little more than a kindly, conflicted woodland stranger. In The Chronicles of Narnia, Lewis reduces the grit and complexity of Greco-Roman mythology to the "pleasant level of a child's story." Graham and Christopher may be right. At the time Tolkien expressed disdain for the story, he had only heard the first three chapters. His strong reaction—"bad as can be," "al-most worthless," "disliked intensely"—was aimed specifically against this small beginning.

Others have argued that the real reason is jealousy. In his biography of Tolkien, Carpenter explains that Lewis borrowed certain elements from Tolkien's work, and Tolkien resented it. His use of "Numinor" in *That Hideous Strength* is one example; the names "Tor" and "Tinidril" in *Perelandra*, which are probably drawn from Tolkien's "Tuor" and "Idril," is another. Tolkien once told Lewis "it probably makes me at my *worst* when the other writer's lines come too near (as do yours at times): there is liable to be a short circuit, a flash, an explosion—and even a bad smell, one ingredient of which may be mere jealousy."

Carpenter also thinks Tolkien resented the fact that Lewis wrote books so quickly while he struggled day after day to make slow prog-ress with his own work. All seven of the Narnia books were written and published in seven years, but *The Lord of the Rings* took nearly twice that long. It may be that Tolkien envied Lewis for his speed and fluency. Or it may be that Tolkien's discomfort with Lewis's haste was not jealousy but rather the conviction that these stories were carelessly constructed and littered with gaps and inconsistencies.

It may be that the mixing of mythologies, or jealousy, or carelessness, or some combination of these concerns, accounts for Tolkien's strong negative reaction. There is evidence for all of them; all are plausible. But in his article "Disparaging Narnia," Josh B. Long points out that we have only one comment directly from Tolkien stating a specific reason for not liking these books. It comes from an unpublished letter, written in 1971. In it, Tolkien tells a reader, "I am glad you have discovered *Nar-nia*. These stories are deservedly very popular; but since you ask if I like them I am afraid the answer is *No*. I do *not* like 'allegory', and least of all religious allegory of this kind. But that is a difference of taste which we both recognized and did not interfere with our friendship."

It is well known that Tolkien disliked allegory. He is quite clear on the matter. He writes, "I cordially dislike allegory in all its manifestations, and always have done so since I grew old and wary enough to detect its presence." Elsewhere he says, "My mind does not work allegorically." And once more: "Allegory is entirely foreign to my thought."

Straightforward enough. But here, too, there is a complicating factor. As Tom Shippey points out, even though he protests loud and clear, "the evidence is rather against Tolkien here." Tolkien used allegory in his nonfiction ("*Beowulf*: The Monsters and the Critics"), his poetry ("Doworst"), and his fiction ("Leaf by Niggle"). He translated, studied, wrote about, and taught allegory, too.

Still, Tolkien states directly and unequivocally that it is the allegory, specifically the "religious allegory," in The Chronicles of Narnia that accounts for his reaction to these books. What is striking about his comment, though, is the way this remark contrasts with his earlier assessment. Both are sharp, and both are quite negative. But in 1949, Tolkien said the book was "about as bad as can be." In 1971, he affirmed that the book was "deservedly very popular," even though personally he didn't care for it.

One small biographical detail supports the notion that Tolkien had a change of heart. When his granddaughter Joanna came to visit, he handed her a small pile of books from his bookshelf, including Mary Norton's *The Borrowers*, Andrew Lang's fairy stories, and Lewis's Narnia books. He recommended them all and urged her to read them.

Apparently, Tolkien's assessment was revised. As Long explains it, "Tolkien remained indifferent to Narnia, but conceded that there was value in the books for others."

At the age of 72, Tolkien writes, "It is sad that 'Narnia' and all that part of C. S. L.'s work should remain outside the range of my sympathy." It came down to a matter of personal taste. He is not scornful, angry, critical, or contemptuous. He is simply sad that he is unable to appreciate his friend's work.

Denigrating *The Lord of the Rings*

When it comes to arguing and criticizing, the Inklings present us with a paradox. There is a powerful sense of play and sheer pleasure in the "thrust and parry" of intellectual combat. There are many, many works (poems, plays, novels, essays, lectures, and more) that were strengthened, saved, or significantly improved by the hard-hitting criticism of the group.

But feelings did get hurt. Toes got stepped on. Whether they were giving advice or receiving it, they didn't always get it right. That is nowhere more evident than with the one book most at the heart of the work of the Inklings.

Tolkien began *The Lord of the Rings* in December of 1937, and he completed the typescript in 1949. That means Tolkien was writing his "new Hobbit" for most of the time that the Inklings were meeting. The book occupied a prominent place, year after year, in the course of their meetings. While the group was generally enthusiastic about it, there were dissenting voices.

John Wain, who complained about a lot of things, complained about this, too. Wain writes, "When Tolkien came through the door at a meeting of the Inklings with a bulging jacket pocket, I winced because I knew we were in for a slab of Gandalf and Bilbo Baggins and the rest of it. I wished him no harm, but would have preferred him to keep his daydreams within bounds and not inflict them on us." When Wain was asked what he thought of Middle-earth, he replied, "The fact is that I don't think anything of it. It has, and had, nothing to say to me. It presents no picture of human life that I can recognize."

There are others who agreed with him. Owen Barfield is reported to have said, "I know this wouldn't be a popular thing, but I just can't get into that *Lord of the Rings* trilogy. I cannot finish it. I just can't get through it." R. E. Havard remembers struggling "to pick up the thread of the story" when he first heard *The Lord of the Rings* read out loud. He borrowed the typescript copy and found that, reading it at his own pace, he was able to "savor its compulsive character." "Still," he writes, "there have always been those who have found it hard to take."

Although Wain, Barfield, and Havard all struggled with the book, Hugo Dyson was by far its most outspoken critic. To some extent, this is Dyson's claim to fame. David Bratman puts it strongly: "If Hugo Dyson is remembered for one thing by Inklings readers, it's as the guy who didn't like *The Lord of the Rings*." Others clearly agree. A. N. Wilson says that Dyson "felt a marked antipathy to Tolkien's writings." And Joe R. Christopher has referred to Dyson as "the anti-resonator."

Why such emphatic statements? It is not just that Dyson was loud in his manner and derogatory in his comments. By the spring of 1947, Dyson had become so fed up with *The Lord of the Rings* that he began to exercise a kind of "veto" against any more readings.

Things got so bad that if Dyson was present at an Inklings meeting, Tolkien would not read. And if Dyson arrived late and a reading was already in progress, Tolkien would stop and put the manuscript away.

Stories about Dyson's vehement objection to *The Lord of the Rings* have circulated for years. Perhaps the best authority on the matter is Christopher Tolkien. In one of the few firsthand accounts of this conflict, he describes the situation this way:

> Well, I should mention the very important figure of Hugo Dyson, who was an English don, English Literature at Oxford. Brilliant, vastly entertaining man who didn't like *The Lord of the Rings*. I remember this very vividly, my father's pain, his shyness, which couldn't take Hugo's extremely rumbustious approach. Hugo wanted fun, jokes, witticisms, lots of drink. And Lewis, who I deeply admired and loved—he had a strong, a strong manner. And he would say "Shut up Hugo. [claps hands] Come on Tollers." And *The Lord of the Rings* would begin with Hugo lying on the couch, and lolling and shouting and saying, "Oh God, no more Elves." The Inklings was a bit like that.

Evidently, Dyson's impact was not popular—Warren Lewis calls it "unfair"—but the Inklings were not able to coax Tolkien to continue his reading if Dyson was in the room.

Tolkien kept writing, of course, so in the long run, Dyson's carping made little difference to *The Lord of the Rings*. However, it did change the

Inklings. After Dyson began to veto Tolkien's reading, Thursday night meetings began to wind down. In attacking these readings, Dyson was attacking the very reason for the group; in limiting the participation of one of its members, Dyson eroded its spirit. It is one thing to criticize an author. It is another to shut him down. There is a difference between conflict and contempt. Dyson delivered an axe blow to the root of the tree. The Inklings were shaken, and they never quite recovered.

DOING WHAT THEY DID: There are two characteristics of strong creative groups: a passionate interest in the same things and a variety of personalities and diverse points of view. Without the first, there will be no glue to hold things together. Without the second, the participants won't have the benefit of multiple talents and perspectives and they won't get enough help to make a real difference.

But encouraging difference will mean conflict. It may seem that the most important way to protect the dynamics of a group is to strike the right balance between positive and negative, between encouragement and correction. But it is far more important to see the difference between correction that is helpful and condemnation that is dismissive and, therefore, destroys.

J. R. R. Tolkien at Tea

CHAPTER FIVE

"Drat that Omnibus!"

 We've considered praise for good work on the one hand, harsh criticism on the other. In addition to these large categories of response, writers who read each other's work may also roll up their sleeves and offer very, very specific recommendations. This kind of feedback may take many different forms. It may emerge in conversation or be written in a letter. It can brief or quite extensive, direct or indirect, serious or playful. But whatever the mood or the method, when the members of a writing group serve as editors, they offer advice that results in specific changes.

The Inklings were involved with one another's work at the smallest level of detail. C. S. Lewis read and corrected the proofs of Dyson's *Augustans and Romantics*. Warren Lewis read and corrected his brother's *The Pilgrim's Regress*. Charles Williams edited Lewis's *The Allegory of Love* when it landed on his desk at the Oxford University Press. In fact, Williams is the one who gave that book its title.

Owen Barfield (a solicitor by profession) read Lewis's autobiography *Surprised by Joy* with extreme care, looking for potential lawsuits before he cleared it for publication.

When Tolkien translated *Beowulf*, Lewis read through the draft more than once, marking up the manuscript, suggesting changes to word choice and phrasing. Lewis was no expert in Anglo-Saxon; his careful editing was not designed to make it a more accurate translation, but to improve it as poetry. And it may be that Lewis inspired Tolkien to prioritize this project in the first place. At this time, Lewis was meeting twice a week to read Old English with undergraduates. He was frustrated with the translations available to him. In a long letter written in 1927, Lewis writes, "I wish there was a good translation of Beowulf." That's when Tolkien started working on this project in earnest.

Whether or not this outpouring of advice makes a difference depends on one thing: how fluid writers consider their drafts to be. When Anne Gere did research on writing groups, she found that one of the most important keys to their success is "textual indeterminacy," that is, the writer's ability to stay open to the possibility of substantial change. This helps explain the effectiveness of the Inklings. As they met and talked about their work, they viewed each manuscript as a work in progress.

Even their name—the Inklings—hints at fleeting notions, half-formed ideas, and rough impressions. Tolkien explains that they did not read polished, publishable drafts to one another but rather "largely unintelligible fragments of one another's works." They shared very rough drafts, fully expecting to revise them: sometimes adding, sometimes deleting, and sometimes rewriting the material. They might take all the advice they were given or take only one small part. Sometimes, advice simply served as a springboard to a brand-new idea; at other times, it sparked a reaction in direct opposition. In all of these situations, the Inklings were open to the possibility of new directions.

The result was constant and significant change. And Tolkien is the one who benefitted the most from this process.

Laborious Changes

Tolkien is notorious for the amount of revision that characterized his writing process. It is often claimed that Tolkien was not influenced by the comments he received; when it comes to listening to criticism, he has been accused of being more ornery than a bandersnatch. But his work constantly evolved, and the Inklings participated every step of the way. Tolkien's first drafts were dashed off at great speed, and these are the versions he read to the Inklings. At times, they are nearly illegible, breaking off into fragmented notes when ideas flowed faster than his hand could write. Having dashed off a draft, he would rewrite and rewrite and rewrite again. He would continue to produce page after page in order to discover what he wanted to say. As a result, as many as 18 different drafts exist for some of his chapters. The complete manuscript of *The Lord of the Rings* has so many versions that it consists of nearly 10,000 pages; the pages make a stack over seven feet high.

Christopher Tolkien explains that his father built his manuscripts in "phases." Tolkien worked like a painter who first pencils in a rough sketch, erases, then draws again, then fills in a more detailed drawing, then adds layers of color, working from background to foreground to final details.

Tolkien revised much of his text; he also revised many aspects of it. Christopher Tolkien says the biggest changes were made to his characters' names and family relationships, particularly the hobbit families of the Shire. He writes, "In no respect did my father chop and change more copiously."

But hobbit names and genealogies are not all Tolkien chopped, changed, and revised. Concerning *The Lord of the Rings,* he declares, "Every part has been written many times. Hardly a word in its 600,000 or more has been unconsidered. And the placing, size, style, and contribution to the whole of all the features, incidents, and chapters has been laboriously pondered." Tolkien revised relentlessly, weighing and considering every single word.

Even after the entire book had been written, Tolkien pressed on and continued rewriting. He explains, "When the 'end' had at last been reached the whole story had to be revised, and indeed largely re-written backwards."

It is hard to overstate the case. Referring to chapter IX of Book One, Christopher Tolkien writes, "The manuscript of this chapter is an exceedingly complicated document: pencil overlaid with ink (sometimes remaining partly legible, sometimes not at all), pencil not overlaid but struck through, pencil allowed to stand, and fresh composition in ink, together with riders on slips [of paper] and complex directions for insertions." The layers of this chapter are so complicated that he provides a chart to help scholars track the progress of all the various threads.

The story of the One Ring kept changing, and so did the larger context of Tolkien's sub-created world. In a description of his father's background mythologies, Christopher Tolkien says, "It was far indeed from being a fixed text, and did not remain unchanged *even in certain fundamental ideas* concerning the world it portrays." He continues, "As the years passed the changes and variants, both in detail and in larger perspectives, became so complex, so pervasive, and so many-layered that a final and definitive version seemed unattainable." Tolkien was constantly working on the world he had invented. Some of the most foundational aspects of plot and characters kept changing. Even the nature of Middle-earth remained in flux throughout his life.

To what extent did the Inklings contribute to these evolving drafts? Their comments fueled Tolkien's natural impulse to keep polishing and perfecting his work. Lewis writes that Tolkien is "one of those people who is never satisfied with a MS. The mere suggestion of publication provokes the reply 'Yes, I'll just look through it and give it a few finishing touches' — wh. means that he really begins the whole thing over again."

This tendency to rework his text was part of Tolkien's personality, a reflection of his preferred writing habits. And the Inklings reinforced rather than restrained this natural tendency.

New Directions

As Tolkien read his texts aloud at meetings, group members not only encouraged him to work a little harder, they also made specific suggestions. Evidence of these comments remains, and one specific comment, made by C. S. Lewis, proved to be the turning point in the history of Middle-earth.

We know that Tolkien gratefully acknowledged Lewis for his role as encourager, for convincing him that his "private hobby" was worth sharing with others, and also for urging him to continue writing when he wanted to abandon the whole thing. We've also seen that Lewis gave feedback on the earliest chapters of *The Lord of the Rings,* and as a result, Tolkien improved the work considerably by crossing out lines of dialogue, tightening up conversations, and banishing long explanations to the appendices. Even though he preferred to write page after page of "Hobbit-talk," Tolkien shifted the proportions and refocused his efforts on telling the story.

Once he had completed these revisions to his earliest chapters, Tolkien found that he was completely lost. He could not figure out what to do next. According to Christopher Tolkien, the story was "a beginning without a destination." On 17 February 1938, Tolkien writes, "I could write unlimited 'first chapters'. I have indeed written many. The Hobbit sequel is still where it was, and I have only the vaguest notions of how to proceed." The next day, Tolkien wrote again, "I squandered so much on the original 'Hobbit' (which was not meant to have a sequel) that it is difficult to find anything new in that world."

Five months later, Tolkien was at exactly the same spot: still stuck and still utterly discouraged. He confesses, "It has lost my favour, and I have no idea what to do with it." Although Tolkien offers a number of explanations, one thing stands out: he is fundamentally uncertain about the nature of this book. At this point in the process, Tolkien imagined *The Lord of the Rings* as a book very much like *The Hobbit*: aimed at a young audience, built around humor and pranks, and modeled on the structure of a folktale or fairy story. He even called it "the Hobbit sequel" or "the new Hobbit."

He writes, "I am personally immensely amused by hobbits as such, and can contemplate them eating and making their rather fatuous jokes indefinitely; but I find that is not the case with even my most devoted 'fans.'" He simply didn't know where to take the story next.

Then on 24 July 1938, he met with C. S. Lewis. Lewis listened carefully to Tolkien's frustrations with his story. He gave Tolkien a short, clear, transforming piece of advice. Tolkien records, "Mr Lewis says hobbits are only amusing when in unhobbitlike situations."

It was an important insight, and Tolkien took it to heart. As a direct result of that conversation with Lewis, he immediately began to consider a more ambitious purpose. He tried to bring some sort of "unhobbitlike" seriousness and weight to this new story.

The new direction can be seen in the changes Tolkien made to a key scene in chapter III. In the first draft, three hobbits named Bingo, Odo, and Frodo have left Hobbiton and are walking through the Shire. They hear the sound of hoofbeats drawing near. Frightened, they hide amidst a cluster of tree roots, in a little hollow beside the road.

Suddenly, "Round a turn came a white horse, and on it sat a bundle—or that is what it looked like: a small man wrapped entirely in a great cloak and hood so that only his eyes peered out, and his boots in the stirrups below."

The horse and rider stop near Bingo. "The figure uncovered its nose and sniffed; and then sat silent as if listening. Suddenly a laugh came from inside the hood." It is Gandalf, arriving at last after a long and anxious delay. He calls out, "Bingo my boy!" as he throws aside his wrappings.

In the manuscript, the story breaks off at the bottom of this page. After Tolkien's conversation with Lewis, he went back and revisited this scene. Here is the same passage again, as it appears in *The Fellowship of the Ring:*

> Round the corner came a black horse, no hobbit-pony but a full-sized horse; and on it sat a large man, who seemed to crouch in the saddle, wrapped in a great black cloak and hood, so that only his boots in the high stirrups showed below; his face was shadowed and invisible.
>
> When it reached the tree and was level with Frodo the horse stopped. The riding figure sat quite still with its head bowed, as if listening. From inside the hood came a noise as of someone sniffing to catch an elusive scent; the head turned from side to side of the road.

The mysterious figure pauses a while, then shakes the reins, and moves on.

It is clear that this new description draws its details from the original description of Gandalf, including the cloak and hood and sniffing sound. But things have shifted radically. Gandalf is gone; a Black Rider appears instead. The facts have changed, and the mood is quite altered. Once personal and playful, the whole thing feels much darker. Frodo fingers the Ring in his pocket and shudders with "unreasoning fear."

With this new apparition, the tale has turned. The sudden appearance of this Black Rider raises two questions. First, what in the world is this terrifying thing? And second, since this isn't Gandalf, what has become of their trusted friend? Finding answers to these questions will determine the necessary direction of the events that follow.

But not only has the hobbit adventure changed, Tolkien's experience as a writer has changed as well. At last, Tolkien seems to catch his stride. Soon afterward, he reports that the story "is now flowing along, and getting quite out of hand. It has reached about Chapter VII and progresses towards quite unforeseen goals." There is a clear break from the tentative and uncertain tone of the past. Now the manuscript flows along and has taken on a life of its own—*it* progresses, *it* has reached chapter VII, *it* is getting out of hand.

Even the title has changed. From this point on, Tolkien doesn't call it "the new Hobbit." He refers to his story as "The Lord of the Ring" [sic]. It is clearly something new, distinct from its predecessor and moving toward a different purpose. All of these changes occur within a month of Lewis's comment about hobbits.

Lewis himself recognized the importance of this conversation with Tolkien. In a letter to a reader, Lewis says he was the one who redirected Tolkien's story away from the frivolous and toward a more serious purpose. Lewis writes, "My continued encouragement, carried to the point of nagging, influenced him very much to write at all *with that gravity* and at that length."

More weight, more scope, more length. Less hobbit talk and far more danger. Lewis's comment completely transformed the type of narrative Tolkien was writing. But there is an even larger issue: to some extent, Lewis and the Inklings are responsible for the fact that Tolkien produced narrative at all. During the years he worked on the project, Tolkien worked in fits and starts. From time to time, he would abandon the novel and, instead, turned his attention to his invented languages or the histories and extended genealogies of his invented world. He admits, "The most absorbing interest is the Elvish tongues, and the nomenclature based on them; and the alphabets." And again, "The construction of elaborate and consistent mythology (and two languages) rather occupies the mind."

Clyde S. Kilby noted this with some irritation when he worked with Tolkien in the summer of 1966. Kilby remembers, "It would be satisfying to record that I always found him busy at his writing, but that is not true. I did find him sometimes working at his Elvish languages, an activity which seemed endlessly interesting to him." Tolkien was a philologist through and through.

Tolkien observes, "If I had considered my own pleasure more than the stomachs of a possible audience, there would have been a great deal more Elvish in the book." Nonetheless, he once again deferred to his readers. If he had not, the work would have been entirely different. Some writers are adamant that since Tolkien worked "from great depths within himself," he would have written everything he wrote even if he had never heard of the Inklings. On the contrary. Without the group, we would have more details of Shire genealogies, more words in the Elvish vocabulary, and fewer stories of the Third Age of Middle-earth.

Tolkien caught his stride at last, and he continued to read his story aloud to the Inklings. And their comments continued to shape the direction it took.

Fine-Tuning

The Inklings were not shy about offering advice and direction. Some comments were global, but others were very precise. While it is easy to recognize and appreciate the major changes, these little details also tell us much about how writers can work together and help each other. Each comment may be considered a small leaf, but each one is a powerful indicator of the shape and nature of the tree to which it belongs.

One example of a precise change is found in *The Lord of the Rings* in the scene where Merry and Pippin first meet Treebeard. The shaggy Ent looks down at the little hobbits and remarks, "Very odd you are, indeed. Crack my timbers, very odd." In the manuscript, this line is crossed out, and underneath Tolkien has written, "queried by Charles Williams—root and twig." The phrase "crack my timbers" is crossed out and replaced by "root and twig" here, and again in two more places in the story.

Several things are significant about this tiny change. It's true: some of the Inklings found Tolkien's story tiresome and hard to follow (Dyson disliked it; Havard couldn't follow it; Barfield found the whole thing difficult). But Williams paid such close attention that he noticed that "crack my timbers" seemed out of character. It just wasn't the sort of thing Treebeard would say. Perhaps it was too pirate-like, suggesting Long John Silver or "Shiver me timbers." Or perhaps the hint of noise and violence—a crack or break—seemed somehow out of place given the nature of the slow and thoughtful Ents.

In addition, very little pressure was needed in order to prompt this change. Apparently, Williams questioned its appropriateness; Tolkien listened, took note, and made the switch. And he gave Williams credit for it, too.

There are other places in the manuscript of *The Lord of the Rings* where Tolkien writes down a bit of advice from one of the Inklings. In an early draft of the chapter entitled "A Short Cut to Mushrooms," the hobbits draw near to Farmer Maggot's farm. Startled by three "baying and barking" dogs and the loud voice of the farmer, Bingo Baggins puts on the Ring and turns invisible.

They all continue into Farmer Maggot's kitchen, Bingo shadowing close behind. But then the farmer begins to recount an old grudge: "That Mr Bingo Baggins he killed one of my dogs once, he did. It's more than 30 years ago, but I haven't forgotten it, and I'll remind him of it sharp too if ever he dare to come round here."

Bingo can't stand it any longer. He sees this as an opportunity to scare the farmer, so he grabs his beer mug, drinks the contents, and returns it empty to the table. Then he snatches up the farmer's hat and runs out the door. "The hat went off at a great speed towards the gate; but as the farmer ran after it, it came sailing back through the air and fell at his feet."

It is a merry scene, in keeping with Tolkien's original concept for this new Hobbit book. But Christopher Tolkien noted that there was an inconsistency in this part of the story. He pointed it out. His father wrote in the margin: "Christopher queries—why was not *hat* invisible if Bingo's clothes were?"

Tolkien tried to solve the problem. He reworked the passage several times, first by substituting a jug for the hat, then by adding a rather clunky explanation. In the end, he dropped the troublesome scene altogether. Christopher Tolkien was disappointed. He notes, "I was greatly delighted by the story of Bingo's turning the tables on Farmer Maggot." Then he adds, "I was much opposed to its loss."

Christopher was also opposed to the loss of Odo, one of the hobbits who travelled with Gandalf in the early drafts of *Fellowship*. Tolkien apparently decided there were too many hobbits in this section of the story, so he changed their names and reduced their number. "Christopher wants Odo kept," wrote Tolkien on the manuscript. But Odo was dropped, though much of his grumpy, impatient personality was incorporated into Fatty Bolger and much of his role was assigned to Peregrin Took.

These examples from Tolkien are not the only times that an Inkling has written the name of another Inkling in the margin of a manuscript. We find it again in a draft of "The Figure of Arthur," a scholarly essay written by Charles Williams. In one of the more memorable descriptions of a reading by an Inkling, Lewis explains how he and Tolkien ("The Professor") met in his rooms at Magdalen to hear the first two chapters read aloud.

> Picture to yourself, then, an upstairs sitting-room with windows looking north into the "grove" of Magdalen College on a sunshiny Monday Morning in vacation at about ten o'clock. The Professor and I, both on the chesterfield, lit our pipes and stretched out our legs. Williams in the arm-chair opposite to us threw his cigarette into the grate, took up a pile of the extremely small, loose sheets on which he habitually wrote—they came, I think, from a twopenny pad for memoranda, and began. . . .

In his essay, Williams discusses the phrase "Give us this day our daily bread" from the Lord's Prayer. Here, in the margin of the manuscript, the name "Tolkien" has been written in pencil. Lewis provides a footnote to explain that Tolkien interrupted the reading at this point in the chapter and "raised some philological questions about the meaning of ἐπιούσιον [daily]." Lewis speculates that Williams "intended to discuss the matter with him more fully on some later occasion." Williams died before he finished the book, so there is no further record of philological conversations or editorial changes. But the reading, and the interruption, question, and attribution are all documented.

Williams penciled another comment in the margins of this manuscript that can be traced to another interruption by an Inkling. In a section discussing the sources used by Geoffrey of Monmouth, Williams dismisses the possibility of "some intermediary tale which is now wholly lost." Lewis writes, "At this point I interrupted the reading to suggest that the view taken by A. Griscom (*The Historia Regum Britan-*

niae of Geoffrey of Monmouth, London, 1929) was different. The single word 'Griscom' pencilled on the MS. doubtless means that Williams intended to give the matter further consideration."

Everything about this exchange is typical of the way the Inklings edited one another's work. The author reads aloud from a rough draft, handwritten on loose sheets of paper. The reader is interrupted; here, Lewis jumps in and offers a specific suggestion. The author listens, then jots a quick note on the manuscript. The note is brief and somewhat cryptic. It is also completely unattributed. This example helps paint a picture of how the Inklings interacted when they gathered, whether in groups of two, or three, or in the larger Thursday meetings. It suggests that other marginalia may have come from similar comments and advice.

In considering these editing changes, we also see a hint of the wide range of feedback these men offered one another. An awkward phrase is corrected, a philological question is raised, a biblical passage is explicated, and an additional source that offers a contrasting point of view is recommended. As the following illustrations will show, this is only a small sample of the kinds of feedback they shared.

The Lay of Leithian

Tolkien began his work on "the new Hobbit" in 1937, and by then, the Inklings were meeting frequently. Feedback was extensive as the members talked together late into the night. But earlier, before regular meetings were established, Tolkien shared *The Lay of Leithian* with Lewis, and this is one of the few cases where we have an extended *written* commentary from one Inkling to another. In fact, in this instance we have an unusually complete record of the poem's development. We can study Tolkien's original rough drafts, we can read the full text of Lewis's suggestions, and then we can compare both to Tolkien's revisions. A close look at this exchange reveals much about how carefully the Inklings edited one another's work.

The Lay of Leithian is a long narrative poem, more than four thousand lines, written in octosyllabic couplets. It holds a significant place in Inklings history, for this is the poem Tolkien showed to Lewis in December of 1929, the one that led to the deepening of their friendship, and before long, the founding of the Inklings.

After Tolkien and Lewis first discussed the poem, Lewis took it home and read it with great care. The next day, he wrote a brief and enthusiastic letter, insisting that the work deserves a wide audience. This was the kind of encouragement that, as we have seen, meant a great deal to Tolkien.

Sometime later, Lewis responded to *The Lay of Leithian* again. This time, rather than giving a short note or a brief word of encouragement, Lewis wrote fourteen pages of detailed, line-by-line criticism. The form of Lewis's commentary is ingenious, for it is written as if a series of scholarly experts have published an article in a journal called *Gestudien*, critiquing variant manuscripts of an ancient poem. He names his imaginary experts Peabody, Pumpernickel, Schuffer, Bentley, and Schick. Lewis offers line-by-line commentary on Tolkien's poem (and also makes fun of typical academic discourse) by writing dialogue for these characters using exaggerated academic jargon.

For example, at one point Peabody observes, "The combination of extreme simplicity, with convincing truth of psychology, and the pathos which, without comment, makes us aware that Gorlim is at once pardonable and unpardonable, render this part of the story extremely affecting." In a different section, Shuffer decides, "My own conclusion is that *if* the assonance in the *textus receptus* is correct, the same phenomenon must originally have occurred often, and have been suppressed elsewhere by the scribes."

By using this form of criticism, Lewis mocks the obscure vocabulary one can find in academic journals. He also creates multiple voices, much like the conversation you find when writers gather in a writing group.

It also allows Lewis to claim that the weak passages of the poem are not poorly written poetry; instead, they are merely unfortunate corruptions of the original manuscript. For example, twenty lines of the poem are marked with this note: "The passage, as it stands, is seriously corrupt, though the beauty of the original can still be discerned." As Christopher Tolkien notes, this pretense "entertainingly took the sting from some sharply expressed judgements," and that made the criticism easier for Tolkien to take.

At one point, the commentary reads, "Many scholars have rejected lines 1–8 altogether as unworthy of the poet." This is one of two places where Lewis labels lines as "unworthy." And, in both cases, Tolkien completely rewrote these sections. Lewis also complains that there are too many monosyllabic lines, and the revised versions show that Tolkien attempted to eliminate them, too.

Other criticisms of the poem are more precise. For example, he comments that Tolkien's use of "did" to fill out a line is clumsy. Tolkien eliminates this three times in the poem ("did fall," "did flutter," and "did waver").

Overall, many, many specific lines are changed. Here are a few examples:

Lewis called this weak: "who had this king once held in scorn"
Tolkien changed it to this: "who once a prince of Men was born"

Lewis called this Latinised: "or ask how she escaping came"
Tolkien changed it to this: "or ask how she escaped and came"

Lewis called this harsh: "bewildered, enchanted and forlorn"
Tolkien changed it to this: "enchanted, wildered, and forlorn"

Lewis criticized Tolkien's poem line by line, making suggestions that improved the rhythms of the poem and provided better imagery. But he did even more. He completely rewrote a number of passages, claiming that these alternatives were the "true" or "authentic" work of the poet. This shows remarkable boldness. It is one thing to suggest that an author change a weak line or avoid monosyllabic constructions; it is quite another to personally rewrite the verse. Yet Lewis did just that. And the extent to which Tolkien incorporated Lewis's ideas is striking.

The following examples show some of these changes step by step. First is the line as Tolkien originally wrote it, then the line as Lewis suggested it ought to be written. Finally, in each case, is the line as it appeared in Tolkien's revision:

Original Tolkien: "of mortal feaster ever heard"
Lewis suggestion: "Of mortal men at feast has heard"
Revised Tolkien: "of mortal Men at feast hath heard"

Original Tolkien: "his evil legions' marshalled hate"
Lewis suggestion: "The legions of his marching hate"
Revised Tolkien: "the legions of his marshalled hate"

Tolkien incorporated specific suggestions made by Lewis, sometimes using them exactly, sometimes using them as a springboard to invent something new. It is a remarkable exchange of intelligent critique and careful revision.

Christopher Tolkien writes, "Almost all the verses which Lewis found wanting for one reason or another are marked for revision in the typescript B if not actually rewritten, and in many cases his proposed emendations, or modifications of them, are incorporated into the text."

Nonetheless, Tolkien did dispute some of the suggestions. Lewis remarks that internal rhyme is always "an infallible mark of corruption," but Tolkien continues to use it anyway. Also, Lewis claims that lines 631–32 ("the dizzy moon was twisted grey / in tears, for she had fled away") made use of "half-hearted personification." Next to this criticism, Tolkien writes, "Not so!!" adding this explanation: "The moon was dizzy and twisted because of the tears in his eyes." Despite Tolkien's emphatic protest, he still eliminated these lines from the poem.

In another case, Tolkien used chiasmus, a literary device that makes use of inverted word order. Tolkien's lines read,

"Where art thou gone? The day is bare,
the sunlight dark, and cold the air!"

Lewis is critical of this figure of speech, writing "The chiasmus is suspiciously classical." He recommends a straight parallel structure instead: "Dark is the sun, cold is the air." In the margin, Tolkien writes in protest: "But classics did not invent chiasmus!—it is perfectly natural." In this case, no changes were made to the text.

Nor did Tolkien accept Lewis's rather peculiar suggestion that the spelling of labyrinth in line 1075 be changed to "laborynth."

But these are exceptions. All in all, the extent to which Tolkien re-wrote his poem in response to Lewis's suggestions is remarkable. Remarkable, too, is the time span involved. Tolkien began the poem in September of 1925; he was still working on it and incorporating changes more than thirty years later.

Rival Wizards

Tolkien does not mention Lewis's ongoing participation in *The Lay of Leithian*. But he does give credit to Lewis for the significant editing of what he calls the "Saruman passage" in *The Lord of the Rings*. Tolkien says that he revised this section extensively in response to Lewis's "detailed criticisms." He also says that the revised version is "much better" as a result.

Tolkien identifies this section as "the confrontation between Gandalf and his rival wizard, Saruman, in the ravaged city of Isengard." There are many, many changes to this portion of the manuscript.

1. A long discourse on tobacco is marked "Put into Foreword."
2. In the draft, Théoden laughs loudly. In the revision, the laughter is removed and "his gravity (at least of bearing) was restored."
3. In the draft, Gandalf makes an unkind remark to Théoden about his age: "It is long since you listened to tales by the fireside, . . . and in that rather than in white hairs you show your age, without increase in wisdom." This remark is "very firmly struck through on the manuscript."
4. In the first draft, Théoden delivers a lengthy discussion about hobbits, explaining that he has heard of *holbytlan*, "half-high folk" who dwell in holes. Then he speculates at some length about the origin of their name. This philological excursus was dropped.
5. In the margin, a question is written, "Shall there be *more* real Ents?"
6. A description of Saruman's voice is substantially altered. In an early draft, it is "unpleasant" and "scornful." In the revised version, "Its tone was that of a kindly heart aggrieved by injuries undeserved."
7. In the original sketch of the scene, Gandalf takes Saruman's staff away from him and breaks it in his hands. In the published version,

the scene is far more dramatic. Gandalf "raised his hand, and spoke slowly in a clear cold voice. 'Saruman, your staff is broken.' There was a crack, and the staff split asunder in Saruman's hand, and the head of it fell down at Gandalf's feet."

8. In the initial version of the scene, the *palantír* shatters on impact. In the second version it "splintered on the rock beside the stair." In the final version "the ball was unharmed: it rolled on down the steps, a globe of crystal, dark, but glowing with a heart of fire. As it bounded away towards a pool Pippin ran after it and picked it up."

9. A cliché "Set a thief to hinder a thief!" is removed.

I cannot link any of these changes directly to specific comments made by Lewis. But we know Tolkien was "dead stuck" at this exact point in the story, and he plainly credits Lewis for providing "detailed criticisms" that led to significant improvement. The changes listed above—shortening dialogue, adding gravity to Théoden's bearing, softening a caustic remark, removing long expository sections, eliminating philological commentary, envisioning broader possibilities for the *palantír*, dropping a cliché—all are consistent with the suggestions Lewis makes in other critiques of Tolkien's stories.

Furthermore, the physical evidence of these changes to the manuscript is exactly what one would expect when an author is responding to the comments and criticisms of a careful reader—a phrase is emphatically struck out, a penciled note is attached on a small slip of paper, a question is written in the margin.

Having said that, it is also important to note that although Tolkien's acknowledgment of his debt to Lewis is direct, it is also somewhat grudging. His comments appear in a letter he sent to Charlotte and Denis Plimmer, responding to their draft of an article about him prepared for the *Daily Telegraph Magazine*. They sent him the draft, and he responded quickly and with grave concern, working hard to correct a host of inaccuracies and misunderstandings. "I am a pedant devoted to accuracy," he tells them. Then he copies troublesome passages from their article and provides a sharp correction and explanation for each one.

The Plimmers had drafted a paragraph saying that Lewis would make suggestions, and Tolkien would work hard to revise. But then they say that Tolkien reworked the Saruman passage in just this way, and he now claims that it is the "best in the book."

Having read this account, Tolkien offers this rather stern correction: "I do not think the Saruman passage 'the best in the book'. It is much better than the first draft, that is all. I mentioned the passage because it is in fact one of the very few places where in the event I found L's detailed criticisms useful and just."

In his response, Tolkien does affirm that Lewis often urged him to re-write and offered detailed and helpful suggestions. This process has had an impact on this specific passage, which is "much better" as a result.

However, the curious thing is that Tolkien says this is one of "very few places" where he found Lewis's feedback "useful and just." Else-where, Tolkien expresses unqualified enthusiasm for Lewis's help and support. A look at the context may shed some light on the apparent discrepancy. Tolkien is responding to an article that has misquoted and misrepresented him. He finds it necessary to write pages and pages of corrections on subjects as diverse as his height, his ancestry, his views on Dante, and his reading habits. The grumpy and somewhat defensive tone is certainly understandable given the nature of the document.

But it is more likely that the date rather than the circumstances pro-vides the key to understanding Tolkien's comment. This was written in 1967, nearly forty years after Lewis and Tolkien began to meet and share their manuscripts. As Tolkien got older, he increasingly denied the par-ticipation of others in the creation of his work. Tolkien says this is one of the few places where Lewis's detailed criticisms were useful and just. It may be more accurate to say this is one of the few places where Tolkien specifically acknowledges the careful editing of his friend.

Changes Here and There

Lewis's writing process was quite different from Tolkien's. While Tol-kien wrote things out in order to discover what he wanted to say, Lewis tended to mull things over before committing anything to paper. While Tolkien produced draft after draft, Lewis completed his work rapidly once he had settled on a clear idea and the right form to express it. And while Tolkien reconsidered every word on every page, when Lewis finished a story, he was restless to move on.

Given his tendencies, some people picture Lewis as a man who sat down, wrote a book, and sent it off to the publisher. Walter Hooper, for example, says that if you look at Lewis's manuscripts, "There is next to no evidence of rewriting or of copious changes." He adds, as if with pride, "You don't have a man revising or anything like that." There is some truth to this, and scholars rightly point to the rapid composition of *The Pilgrim's Regress* (written in two weeks) and certain gaps and inconsistencies in The Chronicles of Narnia (seven books in seven years) as evidence. But even though this view is commonly held, it is still incomplete. Lewis was open to changing his work.

For one thing, Lewis liked to try out his story ideas in more than one form, creating several variations of the same work. This is a radical form of revision, one that allowed him to explore various concepts, images, motifs, and phrasing, and paved the way for rapid composition once he discovered the best genre for the work. *Dymer,* for example, was first written in prose form, a second time in verse form, next as a ballad he called "The Red Maid," and then a fourth and final time as a long epic poem. *Till We Have Faces* underwent a similar transformation: in November of 1922, Lewis recorded that he hoped to write a masque or play based on the Cupid and Psyche myth. But rather than writing it as a play, he spent the next year trying to write it as a poem. Then, more than 30 years later, he started all over again and wrote it as a novel. *Perelandra* also went through drastic changes. It started out as a short poem that included references to floating islands and a green lady. Lewis abandoned the poem, and sometime later, he wrote it as a novel.

In each of these examples, the final version was written very rapidly, with Lewis pausing only to dip his pen into the inkwell. But Lewis had been pondering these images and ideas for years. He had also attempted very different versions before he discovered their final form.

In addition, there are a number of instances where Lewis did substantially revise his finished work. The most extensive example is *The Magician's Nephew.* Lewis began it in 1949, right after he finished *The Lion, the Witch and the Wardrobe.* He abandoned it, returned to it, and then drafted nearly the whole thing. He showed it to his friend Roger

Lancelyn Green, and on the basis of his feedback, he dropped half of the story and rewrote the rest.

Following their initial publication, Lewis rewrote Chapter 3 of *Miracles*, and he produced abridged versions of both *Perelandra* and *That Hideous Strength*. When he wrote the text of his broadcast talks for the BBC, he worked closely with several of their editors and revised the talks to suit his radio audiences. The scripts of these talks were edited and published as a series of short books, and then he edited them again; they were published together as *Mere Christianity*.

There are other examples. He wrote *The Pilgrim's Regress* quickly, and when he had finished it, he sent it to Arthur Greeves along with an extended request for comments, asking particularly for help on any passages "where one word less wd. make all the difference." He sent Sister Penelope the draft of *Perelandra*, saying, "It's uncorrected, so you can exercise your textual criticism on it." He wanted feedback, and feedback made a difference.

There is also evidence of revising on his sermons and essays. The manuscript of "Learning in Wartime" is typical. It shows words crossed out and ideas refined. In between the time when he wrote it and the time he delivered it, more than 10% of the text was changed.

Lewis did niggle over tiny details and factual inconsistencies in his work. One particularly apt example comes from *The Screwtape Letters*. In the first edition, published in 1942, Screwtape advises Wormwood that his "patient" can be coaxed out of the British Museum and, once he is on the street, can be distracted by the sight of a newsboy, then the No. 73 bus, and so on. Apparently, numerous readers sent letters to tell Lewis such a thing was impossible—one simply couldn't see the No. 73 bus from the street in front of the British Museum. "Drat that Omnibus!" wrote Lewis, and he tried hard to find a solution.

In 1959, Lewis began working on a new edition of *The Screwtape Letters*. He planned to write a new preface and add a chapter called "Screwtape Proposes a Toast." He also wanted to take advantage of the opportunity and change the troublesome first letter, so the problem of the No. 73 bus would no longer attract complaints. Lewis listed the possibilities in a letter to his publisher, Jocelyn Gibb: "If you can provide the number of any bus that might be seen in some such neighbouring street, and then emend *street* to *streets* in the last line of p. 24, we shall have saved our bacon. If this is impossible then take your choice of *green coach, jeep, fire engine, Rolls, police car, or ambulance."*

Gibb considered the options and made the most modest change possible: he added the single letter "s" to the word "street." The line now reads: "Once he was in the streets the battle was won." Lewis was greatly relieved at this elegant solution. "I believe we've got it right," he said. One small change, and as Hooper notes, "This problem which had nagged at Lewis for over twenty years was solved."

In addition, Lewis constantly revised his poetry. Cecil Harwood provides one example: when Lewis was told a canto from his narrative epic *Dymer* was "not up to standard, he went away and produced another in the space of a few days." He mailed most of his poems to Owen Barfield asking for detailed critique. He talked regularly with poet Ruth Pitter about the craft of poetry and put high value on her comments about his work. Hooper writes "Even after he thought one was completed he might suggest a change here. Then a change there." As a result, "It was not always easy to determine his final version of a poem, especially if there were slightly different versions or if the poem had already appeared in print."

In general, though, Lewis tended to spend a long time mulling over his ideas, then delivered them quickly. Havard writes that for Lewis, "major works such as books grew from a painful period of gestation. He described this state as being 'in book,' and the process of actual writing as akin to parturition—painful but enlivening."

Some of the time Lewis spent "in book" was reserved for private reflection. But it is a striking feature of Lewis's writing process that he typically involved others as he worked out his ideas. One illustration is found in Lewis's interaction with Clifford Morris. Lewis didn't drive a car; Morris served as his driver, traveling with him "some hundreds of miles" and enjoying "some hundreds of conversations on all sorts of subjects." Morris describes Lewis's writing process this way:

There were occasions when Jack used me as a kind of sounding board when he was trying out some new ideas or some new way of putting an old idea or some fresh outline or even, now and again, some striking phrase. As we might be sitting over a glass of beer, or as we were quietly driving along, he would suddenly say, "Friend Morris, listen to this, and tell me if it means anything to you," or, "How does this strike you?" And if I didn't "catch on" at once, I have known him to scrap the whole idea, phrase, sentence, or whatever it was and then begin all over again from another angle or in another way.

Morris's comments illustrate that Lewis talked over small elements, like phrases, as well as large elements, like fundamental concepts. Depending on the editorial feedback he got, he readily adjusted or adapted or dropped material. He had a remarkable memory. All the evidence suggests that, in fact, Lewis did a great deal of revising. He was able to revise long passages in his head, before he wrote them down.

The way Lewis came up with title ideas offers another glimpse of his interactive writing process. A letter to Roger Lancelyn Green shows Lewis suggesting numerous possibilities and discussing them with a broad range of his readers. He asks specifically for advice on his "immediate problem," which is to find a title for his new Narnia story. Then he explains that there has been considerable disagreement on the issue: "[Geoffrey] Bles, like you, thinks *The Wild Waste Lands* bad, but he says *Night Under Narnia* is 'gloomy.' George Sayer & my brother say *Gnomes Under N* wd be equally gloomy, but *News under Narnia* wd do. On the other hand my brother & the American writer Joy Davidman (who has been staying with us & is a great reader of fantasy & children's books) both say that *The Wild Waste Lands* is a splendid title. What's a chap to do?" Eventually, every one of these possibilities was rejected. The new book was titled *The Silver Chair*.

In short, Lewis eagerly sought advice at every stage of the writing process, but since his composing style was largely internal rather than external, there are few written records to examine. This does not mean he did not solicit feedback or change his work substantially in response to the comments he received. There is every indication that he enjoyed input from others and took their advice seriously. Lewis's stepson Douglas Gresham remembers that when he offered suggestions on Lewis's drafts, he found that his stepfather was "the kind of man who would listen to what I said."

Into the Wardrobe

Lewis's habit of asking for feedback resulted in an interesting change to the text of *The Lion, the Witch and the Wardrobe.* Owen Barfield wrote Lewis a letter to convey several concerns his wife Maud had mentioned after she read the rough draft. Lewis responded, writing to Maud: "Owen has told me about the two main snags, from your angle, in the story. The fur can easily be removed. I am afraid I was not thinking of the fur trade at all, but only of the fact that you wd. almost certainly find fur coats in an old wardrobe. Much more serious is the undesirability of shutting oneself into a cupboard. I might add a caution — or wd. this only make things worse?"

Even though Lewis says the fur is expendable, the reference to fur remains in the published version of the story: "Looking into the inside, [Lucy] saw several coats hanging up — mostly long fur coats." But Lewis did accept the "more serious" suggestion to include something about the danger of wardrobes. He adds a word of warning. When Lucy steps into the wardrobe for the first time, we are told that she leaves the door open "because she knew that it is very foolish to shut oneself into any wardrobe." Not only is the warning spelled out, but the verb shifts from past tense to present tense, making the point even more emphatic.

The caution is repeated when Lucy enters the wardrobe a second time: "But as soon as she reached it she heard steps in the passage outside, and then there was nothing for it but to jump into the wardrobe and hold the door closed behind her. She did not shut it properly because she knew that it is very silly to shut oneself into a wardrobe, even if it is not a magic one."

Again, there is the shift to present tense — it *is* very silly to shut oneself into a wardrobe. And Lewis adds an important point of clarification: be careful not to shut that door, whether the wardrobe is magical or not. Altogether, there are five of these warnings in the first five chapters of the book, all in response to a letter from the Barfields.

Objections

We have seen a number of changes Lewis made as he listened to comments from friends, colleagues, fans, and readers. Sometimes he edited, and sometimes he revised. There are also instances where he took quite a different approach, directly answering a question or addressing an objection right in his text.

Lewis does this several times in *Mere Christianity*. After the very first chapter was broadcast on the radio, letters began to pour in, and from that point on, Lewis makes adjustments right in the text to include their immediate questions, comments, perspectives, and objections. He says, "One listener complained," and "I find a good many people have been bothered by what I said in the last chapter." Even more: at the beginning of Book IV, Lewis writes, "Everyone has warned me not to tell you what I am going to tell you in this last book." In describing the basics of the Christian faith to his listeners, Lewis weaves comments from his audience into the talks themselves.

Another example of this responsive approach appears in *Essays Presented to Charles Williams*. This collaborative book includes six essays, five of them written by Inklings (Tolkien, Lewis, Barfield, Gervase Mathew, and Warren Lewis).

Lewis wrote the preface, and six pages into it, he offers this description of Charles Williams: "Mr. Williams's manners implied a complete *offer* of intimacy without the slightest *imposition* of intimacy. He threw down all his own barriers without even implying that you should lower yours." This was certainly Lewis's experience with Williams, but apparently not everyone agreed with him. At this point in the preface, Lewis writes: "But here one of my collaborators breaks in upon me to say that this is not, after all, the true picture; that he, for his part, always found Williams a reserved man, one in whom, after years of friendship, there remained something elusive and incalculable."

What were the circumstances of this interruption? And who is the "collaborator" Lewis mentions here? Had Lewis been reading a rough draft of this preface aloud at an Inklings meeting when someone interrupted and contradicted him? Was he at home at the Kilns with Warren Lewis, talking with him about this description, only to have his brother offer a modified picture? Did he meet with Tolkien on a Monday morning, or enjoy a visit from Barfield, or run into Mathew? We just don't know.

But someone had objected. And Lewis doesn't respond by quietly revising the essay; he describes the entire vignette, question and answer, right in the text, mentioning both the collaborator and the interruption. He then adds a qualifying statement to balance his own point of view.

Out of the Silent Planet offers the most extensive example of Lewis reworking a story in this way. Tolkien closely edited the first draft of this work. The details are mentioned in Tolkien's letter to Stanley Unwin dated 4 March 1938, a letter David Downing calls "one of the most perceptive brief treatments of Lewis's strengths and weaknesses as a writer." Tolkien's letter is brief and indirect—nothing at all on the level of Lewis's lengthy critique of *The Lay of Leithian*. But it shows that Tolkien recognized the book's quality and understood Lewis's writing skills. It also provides a clear example of Lewis making changes in direct response to a friend's critique.

As was typical of the Inklings, Tolkien's comments in this letter are rich in encouragement. He says the book is enthralling, adding he could hardly put it down. He commends the language and poetry of Malacandra, saying it is "very well done" and "extremely interesting." Also, in a statement that must be considered high praise coming from Tolkien, he says "the linguistic inventions and the philology on the whole are more than good enough."

Still, Tolkien does find fault with the story. He says the book should be longer and the story line better developed. Practically speaking, he says, the book is "rather short for a narrative of this type." As a result, "the central episode of the visit to Eldilorn [sic] is reached too soon." Tolkien also took issue with the style, observing "Lewis is always apt to have rather creaking stiff-jointed passages." In addition, Tolkien found a number of details in the plot that struck him as "inconsistent," a problem virtually every fan of Lewis must admit at one point or another.

Tolkien's criticisms occur at three levels: the whole text (plot), the sentence ("creaking" passages), and the word (philology). Nearly every aspect of Lewis's writing is addressed. And Lewis responded with very great changes at each level. Tolkien assures Unwin that these problems "have since been corrected to my satisfaction." Lewis was by nature far more casual about the details of his fiction than Tolkien. If Lewis corrected the text to Tolkien's satisfaction, there must have been significant interaction and substantial change.

But in addition to all of this editing, Lewis changed *Out of the Silent Planet* in another way: he added a postscript. In it, we are told that although the book is presented in fictional form, the events really happened, and Lewis simply wrote down what Ransom, the main character, told him. The postscript is written as if Ransom has just finished reading Lewis's novelization of his experiences and has written to tell Lewis he is quite disappointed with it.

It is enlightening to compare Lewis's comments in the postscript with Tolkien's criticisms about the book. The voice of Ransom and the nature of his concerns sound suspiciously like those of J. R. R. Tolkien. Ransom is irritated, for example, that Lewis has cut the philological parts so ruthlessly. It is not hard to imagine that just as Lewis demanded more narrative in Tolkien's text, Tolkien may have wanted more philological detail and information about the invented languages in Lewis's text. Ransom is also annoyed that so little attention has been given to the culture of Malacandra, to calmer circumstances when the texture of daily life is clearly seen. He scolds Lewis for these omissions, then adds his own remembrances of the geography, and answers questions about pets, funerals, and the night sky. There is the quick filling in of homely details—of the average body temperature of a *hross* and the nature of their droppings and the fact they don't shed tears but do drink alcohol.

Ransom also describes other subspecies, such as the silver *hross* and the red *sorn*, and then apologizes for giving so little information about the *pfifltriggi*. He says in jest, "I agree, it is a pity I never saw the *pfifltriggi* at home. I know nearly enough about them to 'fake' a visit to them as an episode in the story, but I don't think we ought to introduce any mere fiction." All of these additions serve to fill in obvious gaps in Lewis's sub-created world, and all of them likely address questions raised by Tolkien, who was fascinated with language and enjoyed the details of common life.

Tolkien believed *Out of the Silent Planet* was too short; it may be that the postscript provides more of the kind of information he hoped for. But the form is certainly unconventional—rather than going back and revising the story itself, rewriting and adding to it as Tolkien would have done, Lewis creates an imaginary situation that gives him an excuse to list the complaints and invent explanations and then tack it on as an addendum to the story.

In the postscript, Lewis also addresses a logical inconsistency. The spaceship becomes unbearably hot as they pass near the sun on their way home. Ransom asks scornfully, "Why must you leave out my account of how the shutter jammed just before our landing on Malacandra? Without this, your description of our sufferings from excessive light on the return journey raises the very obvious question, 'Why didn't they close their shutters?'" Is Lewis poking fun at himself for making such a conspicuous mistake? Or are the Inklings the ones who asked this "very obvious" question? If I had to speculate, I would guess that Warren Lewis, who loved vehicles and transportation of various kinds, might be the one who caught the error. This may be one of the reasons *Out of the Silent Planet* is dedicated to Warren Lewis, "a life-long critic of the space-and-time story."

Most personal and provocative of all, I think, is the final line of the postscript. The original wager specified that Lewis would write a space-travel book, and Tolkien a time-travel book. Lewis has finished his task, so, as he ends his book, he seizes the chance to pave the way for Tolkien. Lewis writes, "Now that 'Weston' has shut the door, the way to the planets lies through the past; if there is to be any more space-travelling, it will have to be time-travelling as well . . . !" Lewis ends his story with a challenge directed at Tolkien and designed to encourage him to fulfill the terms of the wager and write the book he promised.

Dedication

Every time a writer revises a draft, fresh opportunities arise for comments and questions to inspire significant change. In a highly interactive group, especially one with a long history of regular meetings, only a small percentage of these will be written down at the time. But as this chapter has shown, there are some cases where we can directly trace a specific change in a text to a specific comment from one Inkling to another. The longer I look at source materials, the more examples I find. But one must stop somewhere. Perhaps some sense of the overall impact can be seen most clearly through the words of the Inklings themselves.

In *Saving the Appearances*, Barfield thanks Lewis, among others, for "thoughtful comments and practical suggestions, which I have used freely."

In *The Sunset of the Splendid Century*, Warren Lewis thanks Gervase Mathew and C. S. Lewis "for their patience in listening to several chapters of it in manuscript." Warren Lewis also thanks Mathew for reading the manuscript of *Assault on Olympus* and making "useful suggestions."

In *The Parlement of Foules: An Interpretation*, J. A. W. Bennett thanks C. S. Lewis and Colin Hardie for "corrections and suggestions."

In *The Allegory of Love*, Lewis thanks Barfield, Dyson, and Tolkien, noting in particular that Tolkien read and commented on the first chapter. In *English Literature in the Sixteenth Century, Excluding Drama*, Lewis thanks Bennett and Dyson "for advice and criticism."

In *The Court of Richard II*, Mathew acknowledges "pervasive influences" from friends including Nevill Coghill and C. S. Lewis, and he names Tolkien among those with whom "minor problems" have been discussed. In his article "Justice and Charity in *The Vision of Piers Plowman*," Mathew thanks Coghill for his input.

In *A Study of Old English Literature*, C. L. Wrenn thanks four of his professional colleagues, including Tolkien, who have "given me not only the benefit of their writings but frequent personal guidance." In *Beowulf, with the Finnesburg Fragment*, he thanks Tolkien, along with R. W. Chambers, crediting the two of them for "what is valuable in my approach to *Beowulf*."

In *The Poet Chaucer*, Coghill acknowledges Mathew and Dyson, among others, for "their patient reading of this book before it was printed, and for many wise and learned suggestions they have made and I have adopted."

As we will see in the next chapters, collaborative works, references in their books and articles, poems and fictional characters, and other textual evidence round out the picture of creative participation and significant influence. But here, in this quick sampling of dedications, we see credit and gratitude expressed by seven different Inklings concerning eleven different titles. They acknowledge a whole range of thoughtful comments, practical suggestions, advice, criticism, input, guidance, corrections, and influence.

In summary, Lewis has this to say about the influence of the group: "*All Hallows' Eve* and my own *Perelandra* (as well as Professor Tolkien's unfinished sequel to the *Hobbit*) had all been read aloud, each chapter as it was written." And he adds with certainty, "They owe a good deal to the hard-hitting criticism of the circle." It is a sweeping statement, and I, for one, believe him.

DOING WHAT THEY DID: There is an art to giving feedback. It is common for critics to offer diagnoses: *This is boring. This is choppy. This character isn't working. The storyline is predictable. The scansion is off.* It is often more helpful to offer specific suggestions: *Shorten the dialogue. Pick up the pace. Combine these three paragraphs. Invert these two lines.* Envision a possibility they may not have considered. Or suggest an alternative they may not have thought of.

There is also an art to receiving advice. Suggestions may be most helpful while the paint is still wet and the ink hasn't dried. Inviting feedback early can make a big difference.

And, ultimately, it is important to remember that the word "author" is related to the word "authority." The choice to accept, or reject, or modify the advice that is offered always remains under the author's control.

Warren Lewis at the Kilns

CHAPTER SIX

Mystical Caboodle

 Collaboration can be difficult to define. How much involvement is necessary for someone to be considered a collaborator? We've seen that the Inklings worked together in many different ways—providing support, offering correction, giving suggestions—and the word "collaboration" could be used to describe any of these various ways of working together. In this chapter, we take a closer look at examples of collaboration in its most specific sense: as two or more individuals who think up a project and then work on it together from start to finish.

There are a number of important works worth mentioning. Some involve lesser known members of the group: J. A. W. Bennett, for example, edited a collection of essays about the King Arthur legends, and it features a major essay written by C. S. Lewis. Others are strictly academic: Christopher Tolkien and Nevill Coghill worked together to produce three carefully annotated editions of Chaucer's tales. Some books were really just assembled rather than coproduced, including a collection of essays entitled *English and Medieval Studies, Presented to J. R. R. Tolkien on the Occasion of his Seventieth Birthday.*

For many of the Inklings, this habit of collaboration began when they were very young. This is especially true of the Lewises.

Boxen

The earliest Inklings collaboration is Boxen, an imaginary world created by C. S. Lewis and Warren Lewis when they were boys. It began in April of 1905, when the Lewis family moved from Belfast to a brand-new house on the outskirts of the city. Lewis describes the change this way: "My father, growing, I suppose, in prosperity, decided to leave the semidetached villa in which I had been born and build himself a much larger house, further out into what was then the country. The 'New House,' as we continued for years to call it, was a large one even by my present standards; to a child it seemed less like a house than a city." Lewis was six years old; Warren was nine.

The Lewis brothers took over a section of the attic, calling it "the little end room." This is where Lewis's first books were written and illustrated. He invented a world he called Animal-Land. It was set in medieval times and featured dressed animals, including a frog named Lord Big, a rabbit king named Benjamin VII, and a bear named James Bar. At the same time, Warren Lewis was also writing stories, but they were very different from his brother's. Warren Lewis didn't care about the Middle Ages; he was interested in modern times. He was captivated by trains and steamships rather than dressed animals. He did not invent a new country. Instead, he created an ideal world based on what he thought India was like.

Over time, the boys decided to merge their two worlds into one. Animal-Land came to represent an early period in its history, while India became the modern period of that same world. Once they had worked out a rough historic timeline, the boys revised the geography. Lewis recalls, "Animal-Land had to be geographically related to my brother's India, and India consequently lifted out of its place in the real world. We made it an island, with its north coast running along the back of the Himalayas; between it and Animal-Land my brother rapidly invented the principal steamship routes. Soon there was a whole world and a map of that world which used every color in my paintbox." Having worked out these details, the boys named this world Boxen.

Much of this collaboration took place over the Christmas holiday of 1908. They expressed their creative vision in many different forms: stories, maps, illustrations, and essays. There is a short play called "The King's Ring (A Comedy)" that deals with the theft of the crown jewels of Animal-Land. There is also a fairly long biography called "The Life of Lord John Big of Bigham (In Three Volumes)." Warren Lewis even published a Boxonian newspaper.

Boxen is a beautifully detailed imaginary world, but the quality varies a great deal. Readers who are looking for early hints of Narnia are generally disappointed. There is nothing particularly magical here. Most readers find the whole thing rather dry and prosaic. There are long, drawn-out speeches and elaborate political details. Still, the invention is complex, and the work is clever. It shows that Lewis was devoted to writing from a very early age. Not only that: it offers important evidence of the boys' joint process. Joe R. Christopher notes, "Perhaps Lewis's childhood period of imaginative play (Animal-Land) that was shared by his brother (India) prepared him to be an author who was ready to borrow from his friends." C. S. Lewis began his creative work in daily collaboration with his older brother and continued to work with others throughout his life.

Lewis outgrew the tales of Boxen, but when he went away to university, he continued to create in collaboration.

Rhyming Lines

When C. S. Lewis started his undergraduate studies at Oxford, he gained a reputation as a mysterious figure, "a strange fellow who seemed to live an almost secret life and took no part in the social life of the college." Despite this shadowy reputation, a student named R. M. S. Pasley heard that Lewis was a writer and sought him out. Pasley introduced Lewis to Leo Baker; they were soon joined by Owen Barfield, Cecil Harwood, and W. O. Field. A shared passion for poetry forged the connection, and from the beginning, they read each other's original work.

During their first term at Oxford, they planned several long afternoon walks together, and as they walked, they recited and critiqued the poems they were writing. These casual walks evolved into large-scale walking tours—they would commit a week or so to walking across the

English countryside, across moors, through woods and meadows, pausing along the way at inns and pubs. They adopted the name "The Cretaceous Perambulators." But neither hiking nor sightseeing served as the focus of these excursions. Poetry did. Baker notes, "What did we talk about on those walks? Naturally, of first importance were the poems we had most recently written." The group continued on for several decades.

In addition to talking about their poetry, Baker, Barfield, Lewis, and the others made up spontaneous verse along the way. Lewis tells of one walking tour: "We had a splendid evening 'telling a story'—an old diversion on these walks in which each player invents a chunk in turn: the natural tendency of each to introduce new characters and complications and then to 'hand the baby' to the next man, produces the fun." On this particular occasion, Hugo Dyson met them for a part of the time, and Lewis notes he was particularly good at this game of spontaneous round-robin storytelling.

On another occasion, Lewis, Barfield, Harwood, and Field planned a long tour together. They had a very pleasant start, but then they encountered some nasty setbacks: strong wind, steep hills, scrubby camp, and bad food, including oranges of the "tough, acrid, unjuicy type, which is useless for thirst and revolting to taste." Lewis and Barfield responded to these challenges by converting their frustration into collaborative poetry. Lewis writes, "Barfield and I dropped behind and began composing in Pope-ian couplets a satire on the people who arrange walking tours. Nothing cd have been happier. At a stroke every source of irritation was magically changed into a precious fragment of 'copy.'"

As Barfield recalls, part of the joy of creating poetry was making jokes at the expense of their walking companions. Field, who was tall and thin, they renamed "Longus." And they referred to Harwood as "Philocasius," combining the Greek "philos" and the Latin "caseus," i.e., a person who loves cheese. Lewis notes that composing poetry helped them turn a trial into an adventure, and it had done them both some good: "By the time we had walked three miles we were once more in a position to enjoy the glorious country all round us."

On a different occasion, they created another long collaborative project: "That night we slept at Challacombe and composed ex-tempore po-

etry: telling the story of the Fall between us in the metre of Hiawatha."
Barfield also remembers this serial poem and explains that one of the
lines contained a reference to "the mystical caboodle."

And again, on 30 June 1922, Lewis records a poem he and Barfield
composed together: "On the way back we started a burlesque poem in
terza rima composing a line each in turn: we continued it later, with paper, by candle light. It was very good nonsense. We entitled it 'The Button Moulder's story' and went to bed."

The satire about people who arrange walking tours has vanished.
"The Fall of Hiawatha" was never written down. "The Button Moulder's story" was never published, and I could find no trace of the paper
copied by candlelight. Like the other poems mentioned here, it was apparently a light-hearted narrative poem with a strong pattern of rhyme
and meter.

There is another casual collaboration that has survived, however, and
it may give us an idea of what these Barfield/Lewis collaborations were
like. Lewis often composed poems with his wife, Joy Davidman, engaging in "rhyming competitions" as they wrote alternating lines of poetry
together. One such occasion occurred in 1960 as the two of them toured
Greece with Roger Lancelyn Green and his wife, June. While in Crete,
they stopped at a "terrible tourist resort" called The Glass House. "We
were kept waiting hours for a very indifferent meal," records Green,
"and the band blared away deafeningly. Joy finally began flicking bread-
pellets at the nearest musician." As time dragged on, they amused themselves by throwing out lines of an impromptu poem:

> [Jack] A pub-crawl through the glittering isles of Greece,
> [Joy] I wish it left my ears a moment's peace!
> [June] If once the crashing Cretans ceased to bore,
> [Roger] The drums of England would resist no more.
> [Jack] No more they *can* resist. For mine are broken!
> [Roger] To this Curetes' shields were but a token,
> [June] *Our* cries in silence still above the noise —
> [Joy] He has been hit by a good shot of Joy's!
> [Jack] What aim! What strength! What purpose and what poise!

Composing poems and stories to pass the time, to mythologize their experiences, to give expression to gripes and complaints, to provide mental exercise, or to poke fun at one another was a natural part of walking tours and a common feature of Lewis's friendships. He and Barfield, in particular, enjoyed it. This habit extended across the years. But despite this long history, only one Barfield/Lewis collaboration has ever been published. It is entitled "Abecedarium Philosophicum," and it appeared in *The Oxford Magazine* on 30 November 1933. It is cheerful nonsense, discussing (and dismissing) thirty philosophers or philosophical ideas, following one another in alphabetical order. The poem begins,

> A is the Absolute: none can express it.
> The Absolute, Gentlemen! Fill up! God bless it!
> B is for Bergson who said: "It's a crime!
> They've been and forgotten that Time is Time!"
> C is for Croce who said: "Art's a stuff
> That means what it says (and that's little enough!)"

And so it continues through the alphabet, listing Descartes, Elis, Fichte, the Good, Hume, and so on, all with the same light and irreverent touch. If this published work is characteristic of the larger body of unpublished material, it indicates that silly topics and serious ones were addressed with gusto in the poetry Barfield and Lewis wrote together.

These energizing tours were a creative crucible: writing projects and other creative breakthroughs emerged spontaneously, and poetry was made from the raw material of daily life. There is one other manuscript that came about as a result of these playful and highly interactive outings.

Perambulators

One of the most unusual publications to grow out of these walking tours was a booklet entitled *A Cretaceous Perambulator*. It was published in 1983 in a limited edition by the Oxford University C. S. Lewis Society. This little book had its start in April 1936, when Barfield, Harwood, and Lewis scheduled a walking tour. At the last minute, Lewis was unable to join them. So, as a joke, Barfield and Harwood conspired to have Lewis make it up to them by taking a mock exam. They modeled their test after the School Certificate Examination taken by British students at age 16, and they sternly informed Lewis that he would not be permitted to walk with them ever again unless he passed the test and gained readmittance into the "College of Cretaceous Perambulators."

The test consists of three parts. Sixty minutes are allowed for Part I, which consists of ten short essay questions, including, "Why are you the best map reader?" and "Distinguish carefully between a walking-tour and a walking-race."

One of the most complex questions in this first section asks Lewis to write an essay describing "an imaginary walking-tour lasting not less than 4 days with no more than 4 of the following." The list of potential walkers includes Father Ronald Knox, Mahatma Gandhi, G. K. Chesterton, Mary Pickford, Sigmund Freud, Sir William Morris, Lord Olivier and "Tha Dhali Llama of Thibet" [sic].

The first draft of the test also includes this question: "Who were: Owen Glendower, Owen Nares, Robert Owen, Owen More, Owen Barfield, Vale Owen, Owain, Ywain, Rowena, Bowen, Rovin', Sowin', Growin', Knowin' and Gloin?" Although this question did not make it into the final version of Part I, the questions that did are equally facetious.

Part II of the test allowed only forty minutes. Six topics are given for an "English Essay," including "My Favourite Soaking-machine, and why." Lewis himself coined the expression "Soaking-Machine." He writes, "The word 'soak' means to sit idly or sleepily doing nothing;" therefore, a Soaking-Machine is just a comfortable place to sit and daydream. George Sayer offers another perspective on the origins of the Soaking-Machine in relation to the walking tours: "The routine of the walk was always the same. One of us would shoulder 'the pack.' We would walk for half an hour. If it was warm enough, and somehow it usually was, we would then have a 'soak.' This meant lying or sitting down while Jack smoked a cigarette."

Part III is the practical section, requiring first, that Lewis "show reasonable proficiency in the game of Darts," and second, he "read a Chapter to the satisfaction of a recognised Bishop of the Established Church."

The notes explain that none of the Perambulators were the least bit proficient at darts. And the request to read a chapter comes from their habit of stopping at any church they came upon. They would rest in a pew while one of the walkers would read a chapter from the Bible at the lectern.

Lewis responded to all three parts of the test, with answers as amusing as the questions themselves, full of ironic schoolboy lapses in taste, spelling, punctuation, and grammar. At one point, he deliberately taunts Barfield by indulging in the most blatant form of chronological snobbery. Lewis writes, "It is true that [Aristotle] was not such a good philosopher as Lord Bacon but ought we to laugh at him for that, no We ought to remember that he lived a lot earlier when people were much less civilized."

Lewis invokes Aristotle again in answering the question, "Why are you the best map reader?" He explains:

Aristotles [sic] astonishing learning enabled him to discover that there were four Causes—formal, efficient, material and final e.g.-

   i The formal reason why I am the best map reader
    is because I have the best map reading faculty.
   ii The efficient is because I read it best
  iii The material is my brains.
  iv The final is that we can find the way

A Cretaceous Perambulator overflows with the clever and playful spirit that characterized the creative life of the Inklings. Like other Lewis/Barfield collaborations, it has "a peculiarly Oxonian character, a mixture of high seriousness, good humor, and genial fellowship."

Fragments and Failures

Even successful groups have their share of missteps, mishaps, and failures. Creative work and new ideas for joint projects emerged in conversation at work and play, but for one reason or another, some were never completed. In 1944, Lewis and Tolkien considered writing a book together on language (nature, origins, functions). By 1948, the book got as far as the title *Language and Human Nature*. Chad Walsh reported optimistically, "The Student Christian Movement Press, in its recent announcement of forthcoming books, listed a text on semantics, *Language and Human Nature*, to be written jointly by Lewis and his friend, Prof. F. R. R. [sic] Tolkien, but I gather that it is still in the blueprint stage."

This book project was serious and substantial enough to be listed and promoted by the publisher, and many people knew of it. But the book did not get very far. Lewis began the first chapter, writing about seven pages of it longhand in a small notebook he had labeled "SCRAPS." The pages are tentative, with long definitions of what language is and a preliminary exploration of how it relates to meaning.

Lewis's draft of *Language and Human Nature* shows that the book was clearly intended as a collaboration. He uses the plural "we" and "our" rather than the singular "I" and "my." He refers to "the authors" and their ideas. If this small beginning is any indication, the book was not to be written in alternating chapters by Lewis and Tolkien but offered from a single unified perspective.

Lewis made a good start, but there is no evidence that Tolkien worked on it at all. Lewis was frustrated. He writes, "My book with Professor Tolkien—any book in collaboration with that great but dilatory and unmethodical man—is dated, I fear, to appear on the Greek Kalends." He expected it would never be written, and he was right.

Lewis and Williams attempted two collaborative projects, and these, too, were never completed. A reference to one of them is found in a 1946 letter. Lewis had been talking with Charles Williams, and they planned "to collaborate on a short Xtian Dictionary (about 40 Headings)" as their contribution to "a sort of library of Christian knowledge for young people in the top forms at school." They are called *The Thorn Books*, "being elementary as Horn-Books, dealing with thorny questions, from an Anglican point of view." As it turned out, the idea of *The Thorn Books* did not generate enough interest, and none of the books in the series were produced.

Another failed Lewis/Williams collaboration is mentioned in *Essays Presented to Charles Williams*. Lewis explains that Williams "toyed with the idea that he and I should collaborate in a book of animal stories from the Bible, told by the animals concerned." Lewis describes some of the possible story lines. They could tell the story of Jonah from the point of view of the whale. And they could tell the story of Elisha from the point of view of the two she-bears. "The bears were to be convinced that God exists and is good by their sudden meal of children." This project, too, got no further than the realm of ideas.

Joint Projects

Amid these failed collaborations, many did succeed. One such book is *The Problem of Pain*. C. S. Lewis took up the task of writing this book with great reluctance. Ashley Sampson, an editor at Geoffrey Bles, had been impressed with *The Pilgrim's Regress*, and so he approached Lewis asking him to write a book on the Christian view of pain and suffering. At first, Lewis said no; when pressured, he asked if he might possibly be allowed to write it anonymously. Lewis admits, "If I were to say what I really thought about pain, I should be forced to make statements of such apparent fortitude that they would become ridiculous if anyone knew who made them. Anonymity was rejected as inconsistent with the series; but Mr. Sampson pointed out that I could write a preface explaining that I did not live up to my own principles!"

And so Lewis began. As he worked, he read it aloud chapter by chapter at meetings of the Inklings, and they offered many suggestions.

Dr. R. E. Havard had a great deal to contribute to the unfolding draft. Lewis appreciated his input so much that he invited Havard to write an appendix to the book, asking him to draw from his medical experience and describe what he had observed of the effects of pain. Havard was glad to do it. And apparently he worked very hard. Havard reports with some pride that when Lewis saw the appendix, he seemed quite pleased. He also notes that Lewis revised his contribution extensively, shortening it and also editing it for clarity. Havard enjoyed the process and observed, "I was impressed by the trouble he took to get it right." Lewis is the one who read the revised chapter aloud at an Inklings meeting, and it was received with enthusiasm.

The Problem of Pain is Lewis's first important work of Christian apologetics, and it is still one of his most popular. In addition to the insights it provides into the nature of suffering, it also offers a window into how the Inklings worked together, the highly interactive process of initiating, drafting, commenting, editing, changing, shortening, revising, and clarifying. *The Problem of Pain* is, appropriately, dedicated "To The Inklings."

While the Inklings took an active part in many of each other's projects, there is only one book they worked on as a group from start to finish: a collection entitled *Essays Presented to Charles Williams*. As was noted in chapter 2, Williams first came to Oxford when Oxford University Press moved out of London during World War II. As the war drew to a close, Williams prepared to return to his home and family. The Inklings began working on a book of essays to be published in his honor. Lewis explains that he and Tolkien came up with the idea together and took the initiative in proposing this project.

But on the 14th of May 1945, Williams experienced severe abdominal pain and was taken to the hospital. He endured an operation, but it was not enough to save him. He died the next day.

The Inklings completed the collection of essays, but with a significant change in purpose. In the preface, Lewis grimly observes, "We now offer as a memorial what had been devised as a greeting." The proceeds of the sale of the book were given to Williams's widow.

There is little information about how the Inklings went about choosing, editing, and ordering the essays, but it is clear that Lewis played the role of editor. He wrote the preface, edited each contribution, and personally invited two additional contributors: T. S. Eliot and Dorothy L. Sayers.

Essays Presented to Charles Williams displays the skill and intellectual vitality of five of the Inklings: C. S. Lewis, Warren Lewis, Tolkien, Barfield, and Mathew. And its publication helped to establish the Inklings as a "corporate identity in the public eye." Whether or not it truly represents the group, it does stand alone as the only book the Inklings produced together from start to finish.

One more joint project is worth mentioning here: *Arthurian Torso*. "C. Williams & C. S. Lewis" are listed on the cover as coauthors, and the sections written by Williams and by Lewis are equal in length. In the introduction, Lewis describes the rather unusual origin of this book. When Williams died in 1945, he left two major works unfinished. One was a long series of poems on the King Arthur legend. The other was a long history of the King Arthur legend entitled "The Figure of Arthur."

Lewis was well acquainted with Williams's Arthurian work. He writes, "Since I had heard nearly all of it read aloud and expounded by the author and had questioned him closely on his meaning I felt that I might be able to comment on it, though imperfectly, yet usefully." Lewis wrote a long commentary, based on a number of sources: the typescript of Williams's unfinished essay, his conversations with Williams, and his experience in hearing Williams read these works aloud. Lewis wrote at length about the work Williams left behind. This extended commentary was entitled "Williams and the Arthuriad." It was delivered as a series of lectures, revised and then published along with Williams's unfinished essay.

Gervase Mathew notes, "It is almost a symbol of the nature of their friendship that the draft and the lectures should weld so perfectly into a single book, although superficially the technique is very different." In this one volume, we have literary history and literary criticism and another example of a joint project by two of the Inklings.

Tolkien and Tolkien

Of all the examples of Inkling collaboration, none is more extensive or important than the common labor of J. R. R. Tolkien and his son. Christopher has occupied many roles, including audience, commentator, proofreader, and tutorial pupil. He is also an Inkling, the last surviving member of the group. His father made his status clear in a letter dated 9 October 1945, telling him that the Inklings proposed "to consider you a *permanent member,* with right of entry and what not quite independent of my presence or otherwise." At the time this invitation was extended, he was twenty years old.

Christopher Tolkien's name can be found on nearly every one of his father's works, including the foreword to the fiftieth anniversary edition of *The Hobbit,* the maps in *The Lord of the Rings,* and the editing of *The Silmarillion.* Tolkien calls his son his "chief critic and collaborator."

Chief critic perhaps; chief collaborator without question. Christopher's earliest contribution to his father's work was as a primary audience for *The Hobbit.* He was about five years old when he first heard the words, "In a hole in the ground there lived a hobbit." As we have seen, the presence of interested and eager readers is a crucial part of the creative act. This is true of authors in general and very true of J. R. R. Tolkien in particular.

Christopher Tolkien critiqued both the text and the drawings of *The Hobbit* as the book took shape. He was always very concerned with the consistency of the story, and he offers this example. One night, as his father was reading the story to him, he interrupted, saying, "Last time, *you said* Bilbo's front door was blue, and *you said* Thorin had a golden tassel on his hood, but you've just said that Bilbo's front door was green, and the tassel on Thorin's hood was silver." Much annoyed, his father "strode across the room to his desk to make a note."

Though J. R. R. Tolkien sometimes found this attention to detail annoying, he quickly learned it could be used to his advantage. In 1938, he received a letter from a fan in Boston, listing a number of errors in the published text of *The Hobbit.* Worried, Tolkien asked fourteen-year old Christopher to read the whole book through looking for mistakes, and he paid him twopence for every one he found.

Their interaction continued as Tolkien worked on *The Lord of the Rings.* Two of his other children, John and Priscilla, explain that their father "kept in very close imaginative contact with Christopher during 1944 and 1945 when Christopher was stationed in South Africa. In these letters (many of which appear in the volume of letters published after J. R. R. T.'s death) he sent Christopher regular installments of the book as he wrote them, as well as discussing the ideas and problems he was encountering." Tolkien looked forward to sending new chapters to his son. In one letter, he expressed his appreciation to Christopher saying, "This book has come to be more and more addressed to you, so that your opinion matters more than any one else's."

When Christopher returned to Oxford and to Inklings meetings, he took up another task: reading aloud new chapters of *The Lord of the*

Rings. Carpenter points out that "it was generally agreed that he made a better job of it than did Tolkien himself." J. R. R. Tolkien spoke in a rapid, indistinct voice, a quality that hampered his reputation with his students and exhausted the patience of some of the Inklings. On 6 February 1947, Warren Lewis noted in his diary, "Chris then gave us an admirable chapter of the '[new] Hobbit', beautifully read." Some months later, Warren Lewis noted that Tolkien was back to reading his own story to the group, and he quietly confesses, "I think we all missed Christopher's reading."

One of the most underappreciated contributions Christopher Tolkien made to *The Lord of the Rings* is designing the detailed maps of Middle-earth. His work was based on a large number of rough sketches his father had prepared. Christopher's maps are far more than decorative; the process of mapmaking and storytelling was highly collaborative, and each one shaped the other. J. R. R. Tolkien writes, "I wisely started with a map, and made the story fit." And again, in an interview on the BBC, he observes, "If you're going to have a complicated story you *must* work to a map, otherwise you can never make a map of it afterwards." The sense that *The Lord of the Rings* tells a real story unfolding in a real place owes a great deal to the skill and clarity of Christopher Tolkien's maps. They allowed Tolkien to maintain a "meticulous care for distances," as well as planning the travel routes, accounting for terrain, and determining the pace of events.

Christopher Tolkien served as an important collaborator during Tolkien's life; his participation in his father's work is even more evident in the posthumously published work. *The Silmarillion* is one example. As Tolkien labored on *The Lord of the Rings*, he often protested that the stories that have been gathered in *The Silmarillion* represented his real work. In 1938, he emphasized that his mind was "preoccupied with the 'pure' fairy stories or mythologies of the *Silmarillion*." Nearly twenty years later, he was still adamant: "My heart and mind is in the *Silmarillion*." One of the best descriptions of this important book comes from William Cater, a British journalist who became friends with Tolkien. Cater calls *The Silmarillion* "the heart of Tolkien's invented mythology, the scarcely visible roots from which grew the great tree of

The Lord of the Rings, the source of his invented languages, the origin of his invented peoples, elves, hobbits, ents, dwarves, orcs."

Over the years, Tolkien drafted a vast amount of material for *The Silmarillion.* With the completion of *The Lord of the Rings,* he returned to this project, and after his retirement in 1959, he vowed to give it his full attention. But he quickly became overwhelmed by the task. He found himself easily distracted, and he spent his days writing letters or playing solitaire. By this time, Tolkien had become increasingly isolated, and as a result, he found himself increasingly unable to write.

When he died in 1973, he left an enormous amount of material unfinished, unconnected, and completely disorganized. Christopher Tolkien observes, "By the time of my father's death the amount of writing in existence on the subject of the Three Ages was huge in quantity (since it extended over a lifetime), disordered, more full of beginnings than of ends, and varying in content from heroic verse in the ancient English alliterative meter to severe historical analysis of his own extremely difficult languages: a vast repository and labyrinth of story, of poetry, of philosophy, and of philology."

How to handle this vast amount of disconnected material? Christopher Tolkien decided that rather than present all of the assorted fragments of the poems and stories of his father's mythology, he would select the most important ones and arrange them in the most "internally self-consistent" way. He explains, "I had to make many choices between competing versions and to make many changes of detail; and in the last few chapters (which had been left almost untouched for many years) I had in places to modify the narrative to make it coherent." And once he had made these changes, he wrote new sections of the story to fill in the gaps. He notes, "Here and there I had to develop the narrative out of notes and rough drafts." As a result, as Christopher Tolkien acknowledges, "There's a great deal of my own personal literary judgment in the book."

Ultimately, the task was so demanding that he called in the assistance of novelist Guy Gavriel Kay, who worked with him on the project during 1974 and 1975. *The Silmarillion* was completed and finally published in 1977.

The Silmarillion was followed by *Unfinished Tales.* Whereas the goal of *The Silmarillion* was to produce a cohesive unity, Christopher Tolkien's purpose in *Unfinished Tales* was to present the loose collection of incomplete narratives untouched, adding lengthy introductions and explanatory notes.

After *Unfinished Tales,* he continued steadfast in his commitment to his father's work. He sorted through the manuscript pages, and eventually he completed a twelve-volume set called *The History of Middle-earth.* It includes rough drafts and alternate versions of Tolkien's published works, along with scattered stories, poems, sketches, and outlines that were never finished.

In completing this monumental task, Christopher Tolkien used the insight and expertise he alone possessed as one intimately involved in the creation of the work. Among other things, he deserves considerable credit for simply being able to decipher his father's handwriting. He typed and sequenced the scattered sections and provided detailed notes and essays on the various documents. As profitable as it is to have J. R. R. Tolkien's working drafts and background materials, much of the value of these twelve books is found in Christopher Tolkien's notes and commentary.

In addition to these important contributions to his father's imaginative world of Middle-earth, Christopher Tolkien also contributed to Tolkien's scholarly work in Middle English. In 1975, two years after Tolkien's death, Allen and Unwin decided to publish his translations of *Sir Gawain and the Green Knight, Pearl,* and *Sir Orfeo* in one volume. Christopher Tolkien explains that his father "wished to provide both a general introduction and a commentary; and it was largely because he could not decide on the form that these should take that the translations remained unpublished." Christopher Tolkien was called upon to sort through the translations. He writes, "In choosing between competing versions I have tried throughout to determine his latest intention, and that has in most cases been discoverable with fair certainty." He used his father's notes to compile an introduction. He also prepared a short glossary, printed in the back of the book.

There is more, much more. Christopher Tolkien has written a number of important articles discussing his father's work. He worked closely with Humphrey Carpenter as coeditor of *The Letters of J. R. R. Tolkien.*

He continues to prepare introductions and critical notes to enhance his father's publications, including *The Children of Húrin* (2007), *The Legend of Sigurd and Gudrún* (2009), *The Fall of Arthur* (2013), and *Beowulf: A Translation and Commentary* (2014).

J. R. R. Tolkien left a great deal of his work unfinished when he died. What we have of his writing and what we know of his sub-created world is due in large part to the insight and effort of Christopher Tolkien. As Rayner Unwin eloquently observes, "In effect one man's imaginative genius has had the benefit of two lifetimes' work." Without Christopher Tolkien, not only would *The Hobbit* and *The Lord of the Rings* look very different, but so would the face of Tolkien scholarship.

"Well, We Will."

When we think about the Inklings, we usually focus inward, on the ways they met to discuss their books with one another. This is fitting: collaborative circles generally focus on their own creative process. But if a group is successful, and especially if it persists for an extended period of time, its attention will shift, and at least some of its energy will be directed outward. This has been called the "collective action" stage. It begins "when the members decide to carry out a group project aimed at winning support for their vision outside their own network. The project could be a journal, an art exhibition, a grant proposal, or some other task that requires interdependent work."

The Inklings did not invest much energy in collective action, aside from devoting significant energy to publicizing one another's writing projects: promoting book ideas to publishers, writing blurbs for book covers and advertising, and publishing reviews. Still, there are occasions in which they attempted to bring about some kind of political change.

As we saw in chapter 2, one of the first projects that Lewis and Tolkien collaborated on was the complete revision of the curriculum for students at the English School. Several years later, the Inklings rallied again, this time to put forth one of their members, Adam Fox, as the Oxford Professor of Poetry. This is a five-year position, and, unlike other university positions, the Professor of Poetry is elected by popular vote of the faculty. Throughout its history, this position has provoked bitter debate, not only about the holder's point of view, but also about the position's purpose: Should it provide a platform for a practicing poet? Or should it be reserved for a scholar of poetry?

In 1938, E. K. Chambers was nominated for the coveted position. Even though Chambers had impressive academic credentials, Adam Fox was surprised to hear that he had been nominated. Fox reports, "When at breakfast one morning I read that Chambers was proposed, I said without any thought of being taken literally, 'This is simply shocking; they might as well make me Professor of Poetry.'" Lewis, who was seated next to him at the time, said in reply, "Well, we will."

So the Inklings joined forces to oppose Chambers, arguing that a practising poet should fill the position and nominating Adam Fox instead. They lobbied enthusiastically for votes, and Fox won. Tolkien responded with enthusiasm and pride: "[Fox] was nominated by Lewis and myself, and miraculously elected: our first public victory over established privilege. For Fox is a member of our literary club of *practising poets.*"

Some have argued that the Inklings had little motive for this political action—it did not pay off for the group in any tangible way. So why do it? Carpenter suggests that the Inklings wanted to demonstrate their power as a group. It seems to me, however, that the motive was less to flex their collective muscles than to promote their convictions about what sort of person should or should not hold this position.

The syllabus-reform measure and the election of Fox were triumphs of their collective action. But another political attempt ended less successfully. In 1951, the position of Professor of Poetry was again vacant, and this time the Inklings nominated C. S. Lewis for the position. Lewis ran against Cecil Day-Lewis, and he was defeated, with a final vote of 173 to 194. Many believe that Lewis's outspoken Christian faith was responsible for his defeat. Warren Lewis recorded in his diary, "I'm astonished at the virulence of the anti-Xtian feeling shown here." Hugo Dyson reported that he talked to one elector, urging him to vote for Lewis but was told he could not possibly support the election of the man who had written *The Screwtape Letters.*

The Inklings met for dinner after the results were published, and, as Warren Lewis notes, their conversation was "merry" despite the defeat. Tolkien says much the same thing. Although some have suggested Lewis was "cut to the quick" by this turn of events, that is not the case.

As Tolkien explains, "I remember that we had assembled soon after in our accustomed tavern and found C. S. L. sitting there, looking (and since he was no actor at all probably feeling) much at ease. 'Fill up!' he said, 'and stop looking so glum. The only distressing thing about this affair is that my friends seem to be upset.'"

One other election deserves mention here. For many years, Lewis had hoped he might be offered a professorship at Oxford. Then, early in 1954, an offer came from an unexpected direction. Cambridge University announced the creation of a brand-new position, a chair for a Professor of Medieval and Renaissance English. Lewis was chosen unanimously as the first holder of this coveted position; Tolkien was one of the committee members responsible. The Electors wrote to Lewis on 11 May 1954 to tell him so.

Lewis was flattered, but he graciously declined the appointment, citing "domestic necessities." Puzzled, they extended the invitation again, and again, Lewis said no.

Then Tolkien took action. He had a long talk with Lewis. He discovered the reason for Lewis's reluctance was his concern about his living arrangements: he did not want to sell his home in Oxford and uproot his brother, Warren, and Fred Paxford, their gardener. Tolkien wrote to several of the other Electors, urging them to provide rooms for Lewis so he could live comfortably in Cambridge during the week and still return to his home in Oxford on the weekends.

They agreed, and Lewis accepted the position. He was quite clear about the reason: "I have had a conversation with Tolkien which has considerably changed my view." Lewis held the position of Professor of Medieval and Renaissance English at Cambridge for eight years, until declining health led to his retirement. It proved a happy move, and Tolkien deserves credit for it. Through the years they knew one another, from their early meetings as junior faculty members at Oxford to these later years of final assignment and retirement, Tolkien and Lewis worked together within the academic environment and took small steps to make a difference.

In his book *The Four Loves*, Lewis describes the pleasure of working with one's colleagues side by side. In fact, he builds his whole theory of friendship upon this very idea: "You will not find the warrior, the poet, the philosopher or the Christian by staring in his eyes as if he were your mistress: better fight beside him, read with him, argue with him, pray with him." In addition to these examples of warriors who fight, poets who read, philosophers who argue, and Christians who pray, one might add the important and influential interaction of collaborators who write. Together.

DOING WHAT THEY DID: Collaboration has a place in formal meetings, with everyone assembled for a specific purpose, following an agenda, and working out the details of an urgent task. But it also has a less structured side: two children drawing pictures in the attic, a handful of college students composing rhyming couplets as they walk along, father and son drawing maps and telling stories, colleagues exercising their voice in local politics. When you look at the lives of innovators, there is often little distinction between work and play. And when creative people make it a point to spend time together, new ideas and joint projects emerge with little effort, a natural part of the rhythm of each day.

Christopher Tolkien at Home

CHAPTER SEVEN

Faces in a Mirror

 Collaborators might sit side-by-side, working together on some project spread out on the table before them. They may walk and talk together, giving the gift of encouragement or writing alternating lines of poetry or earnestly deliberating a change that might improve creative work. But there is a wholly different kind of collaboration, where, in effect, the playwright walks upon the stage and becomes a character in the drama. The Inklings loved to collaborate this way; as poets, scholars, and storytellers, they wrote about each other all the time.

One poem features a probable but imagined situation: Lewis writes of sitting in a pub with Tolkien, talking about dragons:

We were TALKing of DRAGONS, | TOLkien and I
In a BERKshire BAR. |The BIG WORKman
Who had SAT SILent |and SUCKED his PIPE
ALL the EVEning, |from his EMPTy MUG
With GLEAMing EYE| GLANCED toWARDS us;
'I SEEN 'em mySELF', | he SAID FIERCEly.

The image is striking, but it seems this poem was not intended to capture a moment. It serves as a technical exercise, written to illustrate a pattern of poetic structure. The poem has been published twice, and both times, Lewis presented it with a deliberate pattern of capitalizations and line breaks. It was typeset to draw attention to the rhythmic pattern of "Lifts and Dips" in an article entitled "The Alliterative Metre."

Lewis appears as a character in another poem, this one written by fellow Inkling Nevill Coghill. The two men were students together in George Gordon's discussion class, and they had decided to take minutes of class presentations in Chaucerian verse. Thus Coghill described a paper that Lewis presented to the class on 9 February 1923. In part, the poem reads

> In Oxenford some clerkes of degree
> Were gadréd in a goodlye companye
> And I was oon, and here will yow devise
> Our felaweshipe that worthy was and wys . . .
> *Sir Lewis* was ther; a good philosópher
> He hadde a noble paper for to offer.
> Wel couthe he speken in the Greeké tongue;
> And yet, his countenance was swythé yong.

Another short poem that features Lewis is this one, written by Owen Barfield. Barfield (like Williams) was often discouraged by the limited audience he found for his most profound ideas. He teased that perhaps his real audience was limited indeed:

> To C. S. Lewis
>> My public, though select and small,
>> Is crammed with taste and knowledge.
>> It's somewhat stout and fairly tall
>> And lives at Magdalen College.

Barfield wrote a great deal about Lewis. This isn't surprising, since they were friends for more than 40 years. Lewis appears as a character in several of Barfield's short stories and novels. Barfield wrote four poems about him, too, including one entitled "Biographia Theologia," written entirely in Greek. In translation, the poem reads as follows:

C. S. L.
Biographia Theologia

Behold, there was a certain philosopher!
And the philosopher knew himself that he is one.
And the Word, having become in the philosopher,
    was One God.
And the Word was the Light of his philosophy,
And the Light was shining in his philosophy,
    and the philosopher knew it not.
The Light was in the philosopher,
And his philosophy came into being through the Light,
and the philosopher knew it not.
The philosopher said that no one
    under any circumstance could ever behold that Light.
And when he had beheld that Light, the philosopher insisted
    that its name was LORD.
And his philosophy bore witness
    about the light,
            that it is the Word and the Life of mankind;
    and about the philosopher,
            that he was not born of the flesh,
            nor of the will of the flesh,
            nor of the will of man,
            nor through a command of the Lord,
            but of God.
And, the philosopher did not receive the witness.

Barfield says that the date of this poem is uncertain, probably sometime between 1941 and 1946. He adds this explanation: "I don't think
I ever showed it to [Lewis], though I felt a strong impulse to do so. If I
did, then he paid scant attention to it; if I didn't, it was because I was
afraid of his paying scant attention to it." Barfield is clearly more concerned about having Lewis ignore his work than he is about hearing
criticism.

Tolkien the Poet

Tolkien is so well known for *The Lord of the Rings* that it is easy to forget
that he wrote many other things, including poems (*Bilbo's Last Song,
The Adventures of Tom Bombadil*), children's books (*Mr. Bliss, Roveran-
dom, Letters from Father Christmas*), linguistic studies (*A Middle English
Vocabulary*, "Chaucer as a Philologist"), short stories (*Farmer Giles of
Ham, Smith of Wootton Major*, "Leaf by Niggle"), academic essays ("On
Fairy-Stories," "*Beowulf*: The Monsters and the Critics"), translations
(*The Old English Exodus*, the Old Testament book of *Jonah, Beowulf*),
scholarly editions (*Sir Gawain and the Green Knight, Ancrene Wisse*),
and entries for the *Oxford English Dictionary* (he worked on "walrus,"
"wampum," "waggle," "walnut," "waistcoat," and others).

It is also easy to overlook the light touch and delightful humor that
shines through much of his work, *The Lord of the Rings* included.

That sense of humor is clear and strong in a series of poems Tolkien
wrote about the Inklings. These short poems are all in a form called
"clerihews," nonsense poems made of two rhyming couplets, having a
total of four lines that are unequal in length.

Tolkien's clerihew on Charles Williams is a response to the fact that
publishers struggled to figure out how to promote Williams's rather
dense prose. There was a sharp increase of interest any time Lewis
quoted his ideas, and Tolkien took that notion to its logical conclusion:

> The sales of Charles Williams
> Leapt up by millions,
> When a reviewer surmised
> He was only Lewis disguised.

Tolkien also wrote the following poem about Gervase Mathew, an
Inkling with an interest in a wide range of obscure and esoteric topics, including classical antiquity, Byzantine art and history, historical
theology, mysticism, patristics, fourteenth-century English literature
and politics, African art, archeology, and history.

> The Rev. Mathew (Gervase)
> Made inaudible surveys

Of little-read sages
In the dark Middle Ages.

And of Owen Barfield, Tolkien wrote,

Mr Owen Barfield's
Habit of turning cartwheels
Made some say: 'He's been drinking!'
It was only 'conscientious thinking'.

Whether or not Barfield was in the habit of turning cartwheels, he was a trained dancer, and as such, he was certainly strong and agile. That may be the reference Tolkien intends here. Carpenter adds the explanation that "conscientious thinking" was "one of Barfield's terms for the thought processes related to Anthroposophy." For Barfield, this idea includes "thinking about thinking," that is, becoming aware of how the process of thought influences thought itself. Tolkien also wrote a poem about Dr. R. E. "Humphrey" Havard, whose work as a physician gave rise to his nickname "U. Q." or "Useless Quack":

Dr U. Q. Humphrey
Made poultices of comfrey.
If you didn't pay his bills
He gave you doses of squills.

Tolkien wrote clerihews about a number of Inklings, but it seems he did not write one specifically about Lewis. However, Tolkien did honor Lewis in "Mythopoeia," a remarkable and important poem, 148 lines long. It developed through seven versions, each one a little longer than the one before. One copy of the poem is marked with this dedication: "J. R. R. T. for C. S. L."

"Mythopoeia" was inspired by the 19 September 1931 conversation in which Tolkien and Dyson convinced Lewis that the Christian story is a myth that *"really happened."* Tolkien uses this poem to describe many of the specific themes they discussed that evening. He uses many of the exact same phrases as well.

This conversation changed the course of Lewis's life. It also clarified and solidified Tolkien's concept of sub-creation, his conviction that human creativity is a reflection of the Divine. This poem contains his most eloquent expression of this concept:

> man, sub-creator, the refracted light
> through whom is splintered from a single White
> to many hues, and endlessly combined
> in living shapes that move from mind to mind.
> Though all the crannies of the world we filled
> with elves and goblins, though we dared to build
> gods and their houses out of dark and light,
> and sow the seed of dragons, 'twas our right
> (used to misused). The right has not decayed.
> We make still by the law in which we're made.

Later in the poem, Tolkien expresses this idea again, that we create in accordance with the way we have been created, and this is true even when what we make is somewhat frail and flimsy:

> Blessed are the men of Noah's race that build
> their little arks, though frail and poorly filled,
> and steer through winds contrary towards a wraith,
> a rumour of a harbour guessed by faith.

Tolkien wrote yet another poem about an Inkling, though not a light-hearted clerihew or a philosophical declaration. It is a reflective piece, 107 lines long, written about Charles Williams. Tolkien confesses that reading Williams can be a challenge: "I find his prose / obscure at times. Not easily it flows." But despite the challenge, there is much that is worthy, and Tolkien says explicitly that he is writing this poem for one reason: "to praise our Charles."

In the poem, Tolkien expresses particular admiration for Williams's skill at discerning and describing the supernatural world. He says that Williams is particularly good at exposing the wiles of evil powers: "When Charles is on his trail the devil squeals, / for cloven feet have vulnerable heels." Tolkien notes that Williams offers insight not only into hell itself, but into higher realms as well: "But heavenly footsteps, too, can Williams trace, / and after Dante, plunging, soaring, race / up to the threshold of Eternal Grace."

Then Tolkien turns his attention to Williams's *Taliessin* poems and confesses himself "bogged in tangled rhymes." He finds the "dark flux of symbol and event" to be beyond his scope and says the poetry is full of "half-guessed meanings" that Tolkien confesses he simply "cannot grasp."

But it is not Tolkien's purpose to critique this difficult poem cycle. He admits that he has "wandered" from his point and needs to get back on track. Addressing Williams directly, he concludes that when the whole group gets together, "of your meaning often I've an inkling." He continues,

> Your laugh
> in my heart echoes, when with you I quaff
> the pint that goes down quicker than a half,
> because you're near. So, heed me not! I swear
> when you with tattered papers take the chair
> and read (for hours maybe), I would be there.

Tolkien's conclusion returns our attention to his intended purpose: to affirm Williams as a gifted writer, to acknowledge his important place in their circle, and to pledge his personal commitment to supporting Williams's work.

Creating Characters

Poetry is not the only place where the Inklings show up inside one another's work. They also show up inside stories, including scenes where they wrote themselves into their own work.

When the Lewis brothers collaborated in the little end room and created the world of Boxen, they based many of their characters on the members of their family. As one might expect, the boys used themselves as models for the two kings of that land.

The king of Animal-Land was Benjamin VII, whose surname was "The Bunny." Lewis describes him as rather stout and "not so agile."

The king of India was Rajah Hawki V. Warren Lewis describes him as a young man much like his fellow monarch, "happy, careless, and humourous."

And then there is Lord Big, Little Master, the frog who ruled over both these sovereigns. Lewis explains that he had much in common with their father. The young boys describe Lord Big as a "stout frog of massive build, and on the wrong side of 60. His expression was that of a naturally masterful person, given power by external circumstances, but slightly pompous & inclined to worrey over small affairs: in appearance he was handsome, and was clad faultlessly in the fashion of 30 years ago."

Not only that: it seems the frog has a bit of a temper. In one scene, Benjamin and Hawki arrive late for breakfast, and Lord Big is quite annoyed. "'Upon my word, boys,' he exclaimed, 'I'm sick with hunger.'" King Benjamin apologizes and redirects his attention in an attempt to calm him down. "Well, let's have some breakfast," he suggests. It works: "Acting upon this advice, they all three sat down and addressed themselves with vigour to the eggsoak and curied prauns provided. A curious trio did they form."

Lewis depicted himself again more than twenty years later in his book *The Pilgrim's Regress*. In this allegorical tale, he tells of his own search for joy, and there is nothing particularly subtle or vague about his identification with John, the main character. In many ways, this difficult book seems to be written expressly for the purpose of making sense of his own spiritual journey. The protagonist travels a complicated road, passing "through the mazes of occultism, Freudianism, Modernism, Idealism/pantheism. Finally, he comes back to his starting point: Christianity, "the spiritual home from which he had begun."

Lewis participates as a character in other stories as well, perhaps most clearly as the old Professor we meet in *The Lion, the Witch and the Wardrobe*. It is easy to see many parallels in the description of a big drafty house (rather like the New House with its little end room), a prominent wardrobe (Lewis had several in his home), and children who are evacuated to a country home for safety during war time (Warnie and Jack hosted children in their home during World War II).

Also, according to Tolkien, Lewis was also the model for Mr. Bultitude the bear in *That Hideous Strength* (though Lewis denied it, saying it was "too high a compliment").

Tolkien also appreciated the dynamic interplay between life and art, fact and fiction. He captures something of C. S. Lewis in *The Lord of the Rings*. The character Treebeard makes an unusual *"Hrum, Hroom"* sound when he speaks. This was Tolkien's attempt to capture the "booming voice" of Lewis. The identification of Lewis with this wise and ancient tree-man should be seen as high praise, indeed, for Tolkien's love for trees is evident throughout his writing.

More personally, Tolkien recognized that he put a bit of himself in the characters he is best known for. In an often-quoted passage, he writes, "I am in fact a *Hobbit* (in all but size). I like gardens, trees and unmechanized farmlands; I smoke a pipe, and like good plain food (unrefrigerated), but detest French cooking; I like, and even dare to wear in these dull days, ornamental waistcoats. I am fond of mushrooms (out of a field); have a very simple sense of humour (which even my appreciative critics find tiresome); I go to bed late and get up late (when possible). I do not travel much." Certainly one doesn't need to try too hard to see something of Tolkien in his depiction of Bilbo Baggins, a hobbit who stumbled into an unexpected adventure and then spent his finest days in Rivendell, collecting stories and writing them down.

As mentioned in chapter 2, there are also strong and deliberate parallels between Tolkien's courtship of Edith Bratt and the transforming love relationship between his characters Beren and Lúthien. In a letter written in the last year of his life, he describes meeting Edith for the first time, calling her "the Lúthien Tinúviel of my own personal 'romance' with her long dark hair, fair face and starry eyes, and beautiful voice." Their tombstones in Wolvercote Cemetery read, "John Ronald Reuel Tolkien / Beren / 1892–1973" and "Edith Mary Tolkien / Lúthien / 1889–1971."

Parallels exist, too, between Tolkien and Niggle, the main character in his short story "Leaf by Niggle." Tolkien explains that this story arose from his preoccupation with *The Lord of the Rings,* and his fear that the long epic would never be finished. Tolkien was struggling and anxious about his book, and one day he "woke up with a short story in his head." He wrote it down quickly, with unusual ease. Describing Niggle's work as a painter, and his own writing process as well, Tolkien writes,

> He was the sort of painter who can paint leaves better than trees. He used to spend a long time on a single leaf, trying to catch its shape, and its sheen, and the glistening of dewdrops on its edges. Yet he wanted to paint a whole tree, with all of its leaves in the same style, and all of them different.
>
> There was one picture in particular which bothered him. It had begun with a leaf caught in the wind, and it became a tree; and the tree grew, sending out innumerable branches, and thrusting out the most fantastic roots. Strange birds came and settled on the twigs and had to be attended to. Then all round the Tree, and behind it, through the gaps in the leaves and boughs, a country began to open out.

There are many parallels between the fantastic roots and strange birds of Niggle's painting and the characters and mythologies of Tolkien's Middle-earth. The impulse for the story was Tolkien's anxiety; the setting of the story was Tolkien's neighborhood. He explains that one of his sources was a large poplar tree he could see from his bedroom window. We also know that about this time, Tolkien had injured his leg and limped, as Niggle does.

The most important parallel between life and art was the therapeutic result of the story. The ease with which he wrote it proved reassuring, helping Tolkien overcome a host of doubts. As Carpenter puts it, as Tolkien wrote "Leaf by Niggle," he "expressed his worst fears for his mythological Tree." Writing it helped Tolkien renew his efforts to complete *The Lord of the Rings.*

Traveler from the Silent Planet

In addition to his own fictional characters Bilbo, Beren, and Niggle, Tolkien resembles the protagonist in the first book of Lewis's science fiction trilogy. This is Elwin Ransom, a member of the faculty at Cambridge who is kidnapped and taken to Mars in a spaceship. The name "Elwin" derives from the Old English name "Ælfwine,"which means "elf friend." As it happens, Ransom's academic specialty is philology, and Tolkien himself observes, "As a philologist I may have some part in him."

The likenesses go beyond name and profession, for Tolkien recognizes that many of his own "opinions and ideas" have been "Lewisified" in this central character. Tolkien's daughter, Priscilla, was convinced that Ransom was based on her father. The connection makes sense when we remember that the motivation for *Out of the Silent Planet* was the wager between Lewis and Tolkien—a challenge to write more of the kind of books they liked.

On the other hand, it could be argued that the similarities between Tolkien and Ransom are superficial, and these initial details simply serve to help Lewis get a good start on his story. When Lewis was asked about it, he said that he made Ransom a philologist for simple, practical reasons: in order for the story to move forward with due speed, Ransom must acclimate quickly to the Martian language and culture.

With this in mind, some readers have made yet another connection: they think Ransom resembles Lewis himself. He is "tall, but a little round-shouldered, about thirty-five to forty years of age, and dressed with that particular kind of shabbiness which marks a member of the intelligentsia on a holiday." Words like "unkempt" and "shabby" are common in descriptions of Lewis, while Tolkien was "always neatly dressed from necktie to shoes." Furthermore, it is not Tolkien but Lewis who made it a regular habit to go on long walking tours, and the cold rain and frustration that Ransom encounters in the early chapters of *Out of the Silent Planet* would have been all too familiar to someone with his long years of walking experience.

In fact, Lewis recalls one such occasion in a letter written in 1928. He writes, "We committed the folly of selecting a billeting area for the night instead of one good town: i.e. we said, 'Well here are four villages within a mile of one another and the map marks an inn in each, so we shall be sure to get in somewhere.' Your imagination can suggest what this results in by about eight o'clock of an evening, after twenty miles of walking, when one is just turning away from the first unsuccessful attempt and a thin cold rain is beginning to fall."

The connection between Lewis and Ransom is even stronger in *Perelandra*, the second book of the series. Lewis was "passionately fond of water," and in this book, enthusiastic descriptions of the look and feel of water are absolutely everywhere. Downing notes this connection and argues that Lewis "created in Ransom a character whose convictions and consciousness largely resemble his own." Others, notably Lewis's friend George Sayer, agree.

And, as if to underscore the connection himself, Lewis was known to look up at the sky as evening fell, and, seeing the evening star, exclaim, "Perelandra!"

Yet the character of Elwin Ransom continues to change in the course of the trilogy. By the end, the Pedestrian we meet on page one, well-intentioned but naive and untested, has now become the legendary Fisher King. Here, in book three, Ransom no longer resembles Lewis, or even Tolkien, but seems rather like another one of the Inklings: Charles Williams. Carpenter describes the transition this way: "In a sense Charles Williams himself was in it, in the character of Ransom *as now portrayed:* a man of great spiritual strength, a man who easily earns obedience from his followers but is aware that this obedience may be dangerously seductive, a man of quietness and at the same time of great vigour."

Lewis himself is vague on the shifting identity of Elwin Ransom. When he was asked about the hero of these books, he admitted that Ransom is "a fancy portrait of a man I know." He quickly adds, "but not of me."

Though the identity of Ransom is often debated, these books contain other characters who are easily recognized as friends of Lewis and members of the Inklings. Lewis refers to Owen Barfield twice in the series. There is brief mention in *Perelandra* of a man called "B" who is a follower of Anthroposophy. And then again in *That Hideous Strength,*

Lewis mentions Barfield by name and refers to one of his influential theories.

And when the need for a physician arises near the beginning of *Perelandra*, the narrator asks, "Would Humphrey do?" and Ransom replies, "The very man." So "Humphrey" Havard, Lewis's own physician and a faithful member of the Inklings, enters the pages of the story.

Inklings and Notions

Much of the firsthand information that we have about the Inklings comes from letters written by the members and from the diaries kept by Warren Lewis. There is one other profoundly important source of information about the group: Tolkien's draft of an unfinished novel.

The Notion Club Papers was written in the late 1940s. It describes an informal writers group that met regularly in Oxford during the 1980s. Christopher Tolkien suggests that this fictionalized leap into the future may have been written specifically to amuse the Inklings, as "no more than a *jeu d'esprit*" to entertain them. We know that Tolkien read the story aloud at Inklings meetings, and it is easy to imagine him crafting descriptions and including jokes, puns, references, and jabs designed to provoke a response from the members.

The early drafts suggest it is also designed to critique Lewis's Ransom Trilogy. Just as Lewis had created a fictional collection of scholars, including Peabody and Pumpernickel, to criticize *The Lay of Leithian*, so Tolkien created an outspoken group of writers who criticize science fiction stories, especially stories that rely on pseudo-scientific inventions. At one point, for example, they make fun of science fiction authors who use "crystal torpedoes" to propel their protagonists to other planets.

Like most Tolkien manuscripts, this one exists in numerous fragments and competing versions. The first draft has no title and no introductory frame, but the second draft is labeled "Beyond Lewis/or/Out of the Talkative Planet/Being a fragment of an apocryphal Inklings' saga, made by some imitator." Lewis's book *Beyond Personality* had been published in 1944; *Out of the Silent Planet* was published in 1943. Both would have been fresh in Tolkien's mind.

At one point as he worked on the story, Tolkien jotted a quick list of the members of the Notion Club and identified many of them as members of the Inklings. He says "Frankley" is C. S. Lewis, "Loudham" is Dyson, and "Dolbear" is Havard. Tolkien is clearly inventing names that reflect his experience of these friends, labeling Lewis "frank," and Dyson "loud." And the name "Dolbear"? It is a reference to a drugstore, Dolbear & Goodall, that stood at 108 High Street in Oxford. A fitting name, it would seem, for a local physician.

Through subsequent drafts, the names and identities switch back and forth, and some of the Inklings serve as the model for more than one fictional character. Tolkien is identified with Ramer, a professor of philology. In fact, at one point, *The Notion Club Papers* is subtitled "The Ramblings of Ramer."

But there are also two minor characters, father and son, who share the last name "Rashbold." The name is a translation of the German "Tollkühn" or Tolkien. The younger, John Jethro Rashbold, is an "apparently speechless undergraduate." The elder is an Anglo-Saxon scholar. During one meeting of the Notion Club, Loudham lashes out in criticism of Professor Rashbold and then dismisses him as a "grumpy old bear."

Many references within the story are very obviously taken from the Inklings themselves — puns on the titles of Lewis's works, for example, and a comment on Tolkien's essay "On Fairy-Stories." There is even a joking reference to Christopher Tolkien writing "little books of memoirs" with the titles *In the Roaring Forties* and *The Inns and Outs of Oxford*. But despite these obvious connections, Tolkien warns that these fictionalized portraits are not meant to represent any individual too closely. One draft of *The Notion Club Papers* contains a "Preface to the Inklings." It begins, "While listening to this fantasia (if you do), I beg of the present company not to look for their own faces in this mirror." He explains that the characters in the story are intended to be composites. As Tolkien puts it, "At the best you will only see your countenances distorted, and adorned maybe with noses (and other features) that are not your own, but belong to other members of the company — if to anybody."

Though Tolkien claims that the characterization of individual members is somewhat imprecise, there is no doubt that *The Notion Club Papers* is intended as a group portrait of the Inklings. The participants read aloud from drafts in progress, including fiction, poetry, and scholarly essays. They argue, joke, and quip. And they discuss their works quite candidly. The opening scene sounds like it could be a transcript of an actual Inklings meeting. We are told that Ramer, one of the oldest members, is having a difficult time: "To-night he read hastily, boggling and stumbling. So much so that Frankley made him read several sentences over again." Here, one cannot help but see Tolkien struggling as he reads a specific passage, and Lewis insisting that he read and re-read.

Then Ramer describes the group's response to his manuscript. He records, "When I had finished reading my story, we sat in silence for a while. 'Well?' I said. 'What do you think of it? Will it do?' Nobody answered, and I felt the air charged with disapproval, as it often is in our circle, though on this occasion the critical interruptions had been fewer than usual. 'Oh, come on. What have *you* got to say? I may as well get the worst over.'"

The personal connection is emphasized in this particular scene, for Tolkien has written the word "self" under "Ramer" at the top of this page. Tolkien revised this section extensively, and the new version is much milder than the one quoted here. While the revision may be closer to what actually occurred in an Inklings meeting, this first draft may be a more accurate description of Tolkien's emotional experience as he faced disapproval from the group.

The Notion Club Papers offers us a glimpse of the Inklings as seen through Tolkien's eyes. In addition to readings and critiques, the members of the Notion Club enjoy in-depth discussion about language, reflecting both Tolkien's interests and his point of view. For example, after a long and heated discussion of philology, Frankley insists, "Languages are *not* jungles. They are gardens, in which sounds selected from the savage wilderness of Brute Noise are turned into words, grown, trained, and endued with the scents of significance."

In the novel, Tolkien also speculates about the Inklings' legacy. It takes place forty years in the future, and by then, few people remember anything about the Inklings anymore. But two or three of the members of the Notion Club remain staunch fans. "Jeremy was our Lewis-expert, and knew all his works, almost by heart. Many in Oxford will still remember how he had, a year or two before, given some remarkable lectures on Lewis and Williams. People had laughed at the title, because Lewis and all that circle had dropped badly out of fashion."

He speculates "few even of the Twentieth Century experts could have named any Williams work, except perhaps *The Octopus*" (an obscure play, by no means Williams's best). Not only that, "*The Allegory of Love* was all of Lewis that the academicians ever mentioned (as a rule unread and slightingly)."

Lewis, Williams, and the traditions of the Inklings do not fare well in Tolkien's speculative future. And what of the fate of Tolkien's life work? "Only Ramer and Dolbear bothered with Tolkien" and "all the elvish stuff."

These scenes that describe the meetings of the Notion Club are vivid and engaging, but the story founders. The narrative about the group gradually gives way, and Ramer launches into an extended description (more than thirty pages long) of his dream-visions as a form of time/space travel. Then two of the members of the group, Arry Loudham and Wilfrid Jeremy, begin to actually experience the kinds of visions that Ramer has described. At this point, the story heads off in an entirely new direction, and descriptions of the Notion Club are left far behind.

Tolkien realized his story was turning into something new. On a slip of paper, he jotted this note to himself: "Do the Atlantis story and abandon Eriol-Saga, with Loudham, Jeremy, Guildford and Ramer taking part." Tolkien continued the story, making a creative leap from one plan to another. He wrote roughly forty pages of the new myth, but this, too, failed to sustain his interest. This tale of Atlantis, like the account of the Notion Club, was never completed.

In Memory

The Inklings wrote about each other in more personal and reflective ways, including memoirs and final tributes. In May of 1945, Lewis wrote an obituary of Charles Williams for *The Oxford Magazine*. Calling him an "extraordinary gift," Lewis commends his work as a critic, more as a novelist, but most of all as a poet. In a brief and elegant summary, he ventures to guess that Williams will stand as "the great English poet of this age." It may be said that in offering this magnificent compliment, Lewis's gift for friendship is more evident than his gift for prophecy.

As we have seen, the introduction to *Essays Presented to Charles Williams* must be viewed as a memorial essay. We have also considered the course of lectures that became "Williams and the Arthuriad" in *Arthurian Torso*. One of Lewis's most poignant and powerful poems is "To Charles Williams," in which he struggles to make sense of the way all things have changed since Williams's death. "It's a larger world / Than I once thought it" he writes. Then he wonders "Is it the first sting of the great winter, the world-waning?" Or might it be "the cold of spring?" Having wrestled with the unexpected impact of this event, Lewis is left with many unanswered questions. And the final irony is this: the only person he wants to talk with about the loss of Williams is Williams himself.

Ten years after Williams died, Lewis was still working to keep his memory alive. He joined with Dorothy L. Sayers and published this letter to the editor of *The Times* of London: "Sir. — Sunday, May 15, will be the tenth anniversary of the death of Charles Williams. In his lifetime he became an outstanding figure in the world of English letters. Since his death, his reputation and influence have grown so much that there must be thousands who to-day acknowledge him as a formative influence in their thinking, whether literary or religious." The letter continues by encouraging those who remember Williams to honor his memory by getting together, announcing that special meetings have been scheduled in London, Oxford, and Cambridge.

When Lewis died in 1963, Owen Barfield honored him in two obituaries. The first was published in *The Report of the Royal Society of Literature*, and it focuses on his literary accomplishments. Barfield emphasizes that when Lewis was a young man, his "ruling passion" was poetry. He summarizes Lewis's literary achievement as combining the best of imagination and scholarship. He singles out *Till We Have Faces* for special mention, calling it "muscular and strongly imagined" and describing it as a "striking product of genuinely mythopoeic imagination." He ends by suggesting that this novel may stand as Lewis's greatest literary achievement, as Lewis himself believed.

In the second obituary, written for *The Oxford Magazine* and published in January 1964, Barfield describes the life and legacy of Lewis in much broader terms. He was known first and foremost as a Christian apologist, and also as an author of children's books and as "the originator of a new type of science fiction." Barfield puts an emphasis on Lewis as a scholar, noting "Even if he had none of these achievements to his credit, his work as a lecturer, literary critic and historian would alone ensure him a distinguished niche in the world of letters." Barfield concludes by describing the profound effects of Lewis's conversion to Christianity and his ability to submit to God's benevolent direction, "at first indignantly but with increasing delight."

Throughout the piece, Barfield characterizes Lewis as one who cared profoundly for the needs of others. He mentions two specific examples: his anonymous gifts of financial support to the needy and the sacrificial way he fought against his personal distaste for letter writing in order to offer counsel and encouragement to hundreds of people he would never meet.

Other important tributes to Lewis are collected and published in James Como's *Remembering C. S. Lewis*. It includes twenty-four essays in all, including five from Inklings James Dundas-Grant, Adam Fox, R. E. Havard, Gervase Mathew, and John Wain. In "A Great Clerke," for example, Wain describes Lewis as a man with a hard outer self, "brisk, challenging, argumentative, full of an overwhelming physical energy and confidence," and a soft inner self "as tender and as well hidden as a crab's." In this memorial essay as elsewhere, Wain does not shy away from criticizing Lewis: he says he finds Lewis's personal writing "lame and unconvincing," and he dismisses his novels as "simply bad." Despite this harsh assessment, the overall effect of the piece clearly communicates both affection and admiration.

Havard's most important description of the Inklings also appears in Como's book. In "Philia: Jack at Ease," he tells of meeting with Lewis to treat his influenza and then staying to enjoy a long discussion of ethics and philosophy. Havard expresses appreciation for these long discussions, which reflected their different perspectives and backgrounds: he describes Lewis as an idealist but sees himself as a scientist and a realist. Havard and Lewis relished these deep differences, asserting that their friendship was not marred by them but enhanced by them.

Havard does not idealize Lewis by any means. He writes, "He could be intolerant, he could be abusive, and he made enemies." Such frank comments are balanced by the warm tone; Havard clearly accepted Lewis on his own terms. He writes, "Seeing him so regularly two or three times a week, I came to know him well in all his moods." And, as one who knew him well, Havard concludes, "He was a 'magnanimous' man in the Aristotelian sense of the word."

When Tolkien died in 1973, Nevill Coghill wrote a powerful and perceptive obituary for him. He traces his early years, then summarizes his scholarly work. But the obituary does not merely outline his scholarly accomplishments; it also attempts to capture his character. Coghill characterizes Tolkien as modest, friendly, and delightful. We are told that talking with him was exhilarating. He "spoke in sharp bursts at express speed." It was like holding a conversation "with a muted machine-gun, absolutely on target."

He also tells of a time that Tolkien "donned a green robe, turban and liripipe, parted his beard centrally and gave a reading in the original pronunciation of *The Nun's Priest's Tale* at the Oxford Summer Diversions of 1942." He "had a taste for mild mischief," we are told, and Coghill finds that Chaucer's self-description suits Tolkien, too: "He semeth elvyssh by his contenaunce."

Having elaborated Tolkien's appetite for serious scholarship and pointed out his sense of play and elvishness, Coghill discusses *The Lord of the Rings,* and he offers not only a tribute to the great book but also a rationale. He writes, "It has to be admitted that the reading world is sharply divided between those who are beguiled by these wonderful romances, and those who find them entirely unreadable."

Coghill continues: "Tolkien's romances give delight and hurt not," he says. Then he draws a comparison to Shakespeare. If we are encouraged to read high fantasies like *The Tempest* and urged to "enjoy a magic island and 'believe' in an Ariel and a Caliban," then why should we not also "suspend our disbelief" and enjoy the invented world of Tolkien's *Lord of the Rings?* Why not enter in and believe also in the magic of barrow-wights and orc-blades, Hobbiton, Tom Bombadil, and the tree-top city of Lothlórien?

DOING WHAT THEY DID: Sociologist Howard S. Becker says that each and every innovator works "in the center of a network of cooperating people, all of whose work is essential to the final outcome." This includes many forms of collaboration that take place at many stages of the process, including writing about each other and writing for each other. And it extends even further, to the ways that even the insights we gain from one another become part of the fabric of our own work, as we collaborate with those who have gone before us and leave scraps and fragments for those who follow after.

The Inklings Gathered

CHAPTER EIGHT

Leaf-Mould and Memories

 The Inklings were prolific writers: they left fingerprints on hundreds of documents, thousands of pages of manuscripts, letters, and diary entries. In sifting through it all, looking for clues, what we find are fragments—a quick note in a margin, an offhand remark in a letter. And we are left to fill in the gaps as best we can.

But even if it were possible to track down every last scrap of written evidence, we still wouldn't have the whole picture. What's missing? The text of their ongoing conversations, the comments, questions, and suggestions they made as they talked with one another, casually and constantly, as they went about their days. What new ideas emerged as they walked the streets of Oxford? What random remark lodged in the memory and changed the whole direction of a novel? What project, started by one of them, sparked a chain reaction of inspiration for another member of the group?

Their words, written and spoken, form a complicated web of influences and serve as an outward and visible expression of lives lived in community. As we have seen, the Inklings provided inspiration to start new projects; offered support in times of confusion; shaped the direction of one another's stories; criticized drafts so severely that books were abandoned; changed what they wrote in anticipation of the group's response; initiated competition that spurred their productivity; edited ragged rough drafts and polished finished ones; worked together to produce joint projects; created fictionalized characters based upon one another; wrote poems about each other; reviewed each other's books; and quoted one another constantly, giving variety and substance to their work. They learned a great deal from one another, down to their most fundamental beliefs, concepts, and ideas.

Their creative interaction helps us understand these men and appreciate their work. And their experiences point to a much larger truth: creativity thrives in community.

Genius

There is something rare and special about the interaction of the Inklings; and yet, this kind of creative collaborating is common among writers, artists, and inventors—much more common than most people think. There are two very different ways of picturing the process of creating something new. There is the old-school way: a brilliant but misunderstood genius forges a path, overcomes challenges, and stands triumphant. Think of Michelangelo painting the Sistine Chapel, or William Shakespeare, pen in hand, contemplating the blank page. Thomas Edison inventing the lightbulb. Thomas Wolfe, typing out page after page of *Look Homeward, Angel.*

Joshua Wolf Shenk has written extensively about creative partnerships. He argues that this "lone-genius idea" has become our dominant view. But Shenk quickly points out the problem with this way of looking at creative genius: *it isn't true.*

Michelangelo? He was the center of a group of 14 artists who painted that ceiling. As his biographer William E. Wallace points out, Michelangelo was not only an artist, he was also "the head of a good sized entrepreneurial enterprise that collaboratively made art that bore his name (an opinion piece by Wallace in the *New York Times* was aptly headlined 'Michelangelo, CEO')." Shakespeare wrote his plays while standing on the stage as an actor among actors; Edison's real innovation was designing the first industrial lab where employees carried out research and development, often working side by side all night long;

Thomas Wolfe struggled until Maxwell Perkins came alongside and convinced him to cut 90,000 words from his first novel.

A very different way of viewing the creative process has been gaining ground. Innovation thrives in "the courts of sixteenth-century Florence, say, or the coffee shops of Enlightenment London, or the campus of Pixar." Or a little pub in Oxford called The Eagle and Child. Ideas arise in conversation. Projects emerge when two strong personalities argue, and then, intrigued by new possibilities, agree to work together. A quiet suggestion leads to a whole new point of view. Caustic critique gives rise to a different vision altogether. Two inventions by two different creators take shape along parallel lines, enhancing both. An idea contributed by someone from an entirely different discipline proves the key to breakthrough. Collaborators combine knowledge and experience from wildly different sources, providing needed information that others do not (and could not) know.

More and more, normal creativity starts to look a lot less like a lone genius struck with a single breathtaking insight and a whole lot more like a series of sparks coming from different directions, each spark inspiring something new.

Good Company

When you begin to talk about this kind of interaction and how it enhances productivity and creativity, some critics get uneasy. What about individual talent? Or the painstaking mastery of one's craft? What about those long hours of individual work: the writer at her desk or the drafter at his table? And the solitude and reflection necessary to cultivate deep roots, establishing far-flung dreams on solid ground?

It is true that personal innovation can be enhanced by community. It is also true that a great group depends upon the contributions of great people. We won't get ahead if we simply replace the idea of the bold individual with the idea of the collaborative collective. We need to start thinking bigger. We affirm both.

On the one hand, we notice how often individual talent is enhanced by creative connections. On the other hand, we also pay close attention to the ways healthy connections provide the correction, challenge, and example that enhance the individual talent.

We take a bigger perspective. We take risks and discover how conversation, friendship, collaboration, even conflict and correction, make individual talent better and ordinary work extraordinary. In some ways, this book might be read as an encouragement to rethink the process of invention by stepping back, looking again, and noticing what else is inside the frame when you consider a wider context.

Working out the balance between time alone and time together will vary. So will the relative proportions—silence and companionship, praise and criticism, suggestions and questions. Striking the right balance will be different for different people. It will be constantly adjusted for different projects and change throughout the seasons of a person's life.

That said, connecting with others remains an important component of what it means to be a successful inventor. It should not be ignored. Charles Williams observed, "Much was possible to a man in solitude. . . . But some things were possible only to a man in companionship, and of these the most important was balance. No mind was so good that it did not need another mind to counter and equal it, and to save it from conceit and blindness and bigotry and folly."

Randy Komisar is a businessman who has been experimenting with putting this kind of larger perspective into practice. He has shifted his work ethic away from *efficiency thinking* and has focused instead on what he calls *relational thinking*. According to *Forbes*, in every major decision, Komisar keeps one goal in mind: to surround himself with "the smartest, most high-integrity people." His first priority used to be racing to get the job done. Now it has become "building deep, long-term, win-win relationships."

Komisar says that as a result, he is more productive. Not only that: he is also much happier. All in all, this emphasis on relational thinking has served him well. The *Forbes* article encourages us to consider shifting our approach, too, since doing so can have "a huge impact on our behaviors, well-being, income, happiness, even longevity." And, I would add, doing so can have a huge impact on the innovative and creative work we do.

The scholarly world is also wrestling with the implications of this notion. Karen Burke LeFevre has published some of the earliest and most significant scholarly work on writing as a social process. She offers the following illustration. It is a word picture that is not only a powerful metaphor for the creative process but also might be taken as the theme of this book: "There will always be great need for individual initiative, but no matter how inventive an individual wants to be, he will be influenced for better or for worse by the intellectual company he keeps. On top of Mt. Mansfield in Vermont, there are thirty-year-old trees that are only three feet tall. If a tree begins to grow taller, extending beyond the protection of the others, it dies."

She concludes with this compelling advice: "Plant yourself in a tall forest if you hope to have ideas of stature." That is exactly what the Inklings did. There is much to be said about the good that can come from the company we keep.

Catching That Bandersnatch

Thinking more generously about creativity and influence invites us to step back and take one more look at that infamous bandersnatch comment. The common way to think about Tolkien, Lewis, and their mutual influence is sometimes based on a narrow view, a limited perspective, one short line that reads "No one ever influenced Tolkien—you might as well try to influence a bandersnatch."

But what happens if we take a step back and look again? Here is the larger context of what Lewis said about how the Inklings influenced Tolkien and his work:

> No one ever influenced Tolkien—you might as well try to influence a bandersnatch. We listened to his work, but could affect it only by encouragement. He has only two reactions to criticism; either he begins the whole work over again from the beginning or else takes no notice at all.

Lewis says, "No one ever influenced Tolkien," but his comment is *immediately* qualified. The Inklings influenced Tolkien's work, he says, and they did it primarily by listening and encouraging. And as we have seen in these pages, listening and encouraging are neither passive activities nor insignificant ones.

What about criticism? Lewis says Tolkien would react one of two ways.

Sometimes, he would begin the work over again from the beginning. Starting over? That represents major influence, indeed.

At other times, Lewis says, Tolkien took "no notice at all." This may be true. Tolkien may have simply ignored the advice that didn't suit him. But I think Lewis may be missing something. There is every indication that when the others offered suggestions, Tolkien got quiet and jotted a few notes to himself. Then later, after he went home, he fiddled with the text, thought some more about it, and revised his story. And it seems to me, based on the written evidence, that this happened far more than Lewis ever realized. Like a mythical bandersnatch, his imagination would balk and bolt with a mind of its own. But this more complex picture is far different from the claim that the encouragement, opposition, and suggestions of others made no difference at all. There is a whole lot more going on. We must expand our point of view.

Widening Circles

We've been considering some of the ways creative people interact with their contemporaries. Johann Wolfgang von Goethe suggests that we expand the idea of creative collaboration even further, to include the contributions of those who lived in the past. Goethe asks, "Do not all the achievements of a poet's predecessors and contemporaries rightfully belong to him? Why should he shrink from picking flowers where he finds them? Only by making the riches of the others our own do we bring anything great into being." Writers read other authors. Musicians listen with care to the work of other composers. Managers study other leadership styles, including those from different time periods and other cultures. Scientists build upon other discoveries. Painters find their work enhanced as they grow in appreciation of the painters who have gone before them.

This is not an invitation to slavish imitation or thinly veiled plagiarism. Goethe is urging us to create something great, and that requires breadth of ideas, depth of thought, and connection with voices beyond our own. He asks us to call to mind the riches of others and then to do the hard work of figuring out how to incorporate them into our own unique vision. Consider the extent to which Lewis, Tolkien, and the other Inklings loved books and read widely, including authors from various time periods and stories written in other languages. Consider Lewis's exhaustive familiarity with sixteenth-century literature and his immersion in that early historical community of writers and thinkers.

Dorothy L. Sayers describes the process this way: "Poets do not merely pass on the torch in a relay race; they toss the ball to one another, to and fro, across the centuries. Dante would have been different if Virgil had never been, but if Dante had never been we should know Virgil differently; across both their heads Ezekiel calls to Blake, and Milton to Homer."

Conversations with colleagues. Conversations with those who have gone before. Perhaps the best-known expression of this idea comes from a literary theorist named Kenneth Burke. He compares the act of creative breakthrough to the participation of the individual in a much larger, long-standing, ongoing conversation:

> Imagine that you enter a parlor. You come late. When you arrive, others have long preceded you, and they are engaged in a heated discussion, a discussion too heated for them to pause and tell you exactly what it is about. In fact, the discussion had already begun long before any of them got there, so that no one present is qualified to retrace for you all the steps that had gone before. You listen for a while, until you decide that you have caught the tenor of the argument; then you put in your oar. Someone answers; you answer him; another comes to your defense; another aligns himself against you. . . . However, the discussion is interminable. The hour grows late, you must depart. And you do depart, with the discussion still rigorously in progress.

As this description illustrates, the things we say—or make, or write—exist as one part of a much larger context. We borrow from those who have been there before us. We are sharpened and challenged by those who surround us. And then we leave our mark, our legacy, for those who will come long after we have gone.

Across the Expanse

This "conversation of mankind" extends across the centuries. It may also connect two writers who happen to live in the same city. My collaboration with Joshua Wolf Shenk, author of *Powers of Two*, may be useful as an illustration of Burke's ongoing discussion. Shenk and I have never met. But he read some of my earlier work on collaboration. He called me, and we talked on the phone about creative partnerships, particularly the mutual influence of Lewis and Tolkien. I followed up by quoting him extensively in two public lectures. He then quoted my work in his book. And, here and now, I continue the conversation by quoting him: "Creative work depends on exchanges across an expanse," writes Shenk. "We make our best work, and live our best lives, by charging into the vast space between ourselves and others."

Lewis puts it this way: "Spin something out of one's own head when the world teems with so many noble deeds, wholesome examples, pitiful tragedies, strange adventures, and merry jests which have never yet been set forth quite so well as they deserve?" Then he adds, "Why make things for oneself like the lonely Robinson Crusoe when there is riches all about you to be had for the taking?"

Tolkien also clearly understood this point of view. The true artist does not sit down and dream up something out of nothing; the wise artist understands, even celebrates, the benefits of making connections. Tolkien uses a particularly powerful metaphor as he talks about this complex process. He explains, "One writes . . . not out of the leaves of trees still to be observed, nor by means of botany and soil-science; but it grows like a seed in the dark out of the leaf-mould of the mind: out of *all that has been seen or thought or read*, that has long ago been forgotten, descending into the deeps."

Tolkien uses the idea of the "leaf-mould of the mind" again in a letter to a reader about the origin of the names Gamgee and Gondor. Tolkien explains "one's mind is, of course, stored with a 'leaf-mould' of memories (submerged) of names, and these rise up to the surface." Leaf-mould is wonderful stuff, rich and potent, and no longer recognizable as the thing it once was. Decomposed, recombined, these various raw materials are transformed. They become the soil, as it were, for growing something new.

Elsewhere, Tolkien uses other images to describe what the creative process is like. Out of this rich soil grows what he calls the "Tree of Tales." All of the stories that have ever been written are part of this one tree, connected to the same trunk, leaves and branches "intricately knotted."

He also compares this process to a tapestry, an image that implies the work of many hands, all contributing to one enormous work of art. In describing this intricate weaving, he emphasizes that it is unified and seamless, "beyond all skill but that of the elves to unravel." The fact that each thread is different—different colors, textures, shades of dark and light—underscores the way our differences can strengthen and enhance each other.

Finally, Tolkien uses the image of a cauldron: "Speaking of the history of stories and especially of fairy-stories we may say that the Pot of Soup, the Cauldron of Story, has always been boiling, and to it have continually been added new bits, dainty and undainty."

By selecting these specific images—tree, tapestry, and cauldron—Tolkien emphasizes that each individual creative act is a participant in something much larger than itself. "The powerful play goes on," as Walt Whitman would say. The mood is striking here. Playfulness. Participation. Generosity. Connectedness.

When I have given lectures about this larger and more interactive view, musicians seem to be the quickest to catch on. Yes, they tell me. That's how music gets made. Each performance is a dynamic interplay that arises between the performers and the piece of music and then bounces back and forth with the audience as well. Sometimes, I have even heard musicians talk about how they "collaborate" with a particular musical instrument or they play a song according to the way the acoustics change within a particular kind of space.

Filmmakers, too, readily acknowledge that the story unrolling up on the screen is the participation of the actors and the score, the directorial vision alongside the sweat and service of the key grip and gaffer.

LeFevre emphasizes that interacting with others does more than help inventive people to become more effective. Her words are worth repeating: "Certain acts of invention—or certain phases of inventive acts—are best understood if we think of them as being *made possible* by other people." In many cases, the presence of resonators, opponents, editors, and collaborators does not merely make a project easier, or lighten the burden, or move things along. Often, these important companions are essential to a project's existence. It is true of writers in general; it is also true of the Inklings. In short, none of them would have written the same things in the same ways if it had not been for the influence of this group.

Exchange

This image of creative collaboration seems remarkably new: Steve Jobs and Steve Wozniak tinkering with computers in their garage, Ralph Abernathy and Martin Luther King, Jr., fighting for social change, Francis Crick and James Watson uncovering the structure of DNA, John Lennon and Paul McCartney finishing each other's song lyrics. But creative collaboration is as old as the hills, as old as Story. It is, in fact, older than *The Iliad* and *The Odyssey,* even older than Homer himself, an author whose work brings together a vast accumulation of many generations of oral tradition.

The poet Homer is an ideal image. When we go looking for the heart of the creative process, we won't find it in the gifted individual or in the complex interdependence of creative culture. A synthetic view is required; both are at work. Each individual matters and so does the group. And so does the magic that emerges as new ideas and identities arise when those individuals connect. Composer Michael Lee has tried to explain this to me a dozen times. Here's the best I can do: Jazz happens when talented individuals gather. Jazz happens when the voice of the group becomes more than the sum of its parts. Jazz happens when the music starts to play the musicians.

Of all the Inklings, Charles Williams probably wrote and taught more about this idea than any of the others. The word "exchange" was a buzzword in Oxford at the time, and he used it to describe what it means to live as members of one another. Williams assumed "the whole cosmos is an organism in which all parts are interrelated, interdependent, co-inhering, matter and spirit, body and soul."

Thomas Howard offers the following overview of Williams's theories, especially as they were understood in England in a time of war:

> [Williams] realized that the peace and well-being he enjoyed in England were due to the sacrifices being made by the young men in the trenches of France. In other words, everyone in England owed his life to these men who were laying down theirs.
>
> It seemed to Williams that here was a principle. Everyone, all the time, owes his life to others. It is not only in war that this is true. We cannot eat breakfast without being nourished by some life that has been laid down. If our breakfast is cereal or toast, then it is the life of grains of wheat that have gone into the ground and died that we might have food. If it is bacon, then the blood of some pig has been shed for the sake of my nourishment. All day long I live on this basis: some farmer's labor has produced this wheat and someone else's has brought it to market and so on. . . .
>
> Williams coupled this idea of exchange with two other ideas, namely, "substitution" and "co-inherence," but they all come to the same thing. There is no such thing as life that does not owe itself to the life and labor of someone else. It is true all the way up and down the scale of life, from our conception which owes itself to the self-giving of a man and a woman to each other; through my daily life where I find courtesies such as a door held open if I have a package; . . . to the highest mystery of all in which a life was laid down so that we might all have eternal life.

Williams saw all of life as interdependent upon the sacrifices and service of others. It is a lofty idea. It has been captured in one of the most beautiful expressions of gratitude found in the Anglican *Book of Common Prayer*. Designed for use at the end of the day, we pray, "Grant that we may never forget that our common life depends upon each other's toil."

"The Powerful Play Goes On"

Studying the Inklings as writers in community helps us to understand them better. It also offers us a more accurate view of the creative process. As a result, we describe the past more accurately, and we think about the present more openly. We also look to the future, and we recognize how encouraging collaboration can lead to creative breakthrough and inspire new generations of writers and artists.

Tolkien illustrates this powerfully in a scene in the final chapters of *The Lord of the Rings.* As Frodo is wrapping up his estate before leaving the Shire for good, he goes through his papers with Sam Gamgee and hands him his keys. The keys are physical, of course: Sam is the one who will inherit Frodo's house, along with the rest of Frodo's belongings.

But another "key" is also passed along. Sam stands in line to inherit something else, something far more important:

> There was a big book with plain red leather covers; its tall pages were now almost filled. At the beginning there were many leaves covered with Bilbo's thin wandering hand; but most of it was written in Frodo's firm flowing script. It was divided into chapters but Chapter 80 was unfinished, and after that were some blank leaves.

The big book is *The Red Book of Westmarch.* It was started a generation earlier as a record of Bilbo's memoirs. At that time, it was called "There and Back Again, a Hobbit's Holiday." To these beginning chapters, Frodo has added his own account of the War of the Ring, working collaboratively "with the aid of his friends' recollections."

By now, the title page has many titles on it, seven to be exact, each drafted, then reconsidered, then crossed out and revised. Frodo has taken his turn and written and rewritten the title page. Now it looks like this:

THE DOWNFALL

OF THE

LORD OF THE RINGS

AND THE

RETURN OF THE KING

(as seen by the Little People; being the memoirs of Bilbo and Frodo of the Shire, supplemented by the accounts of their friends and the learning of the Wise.) Together with extracts from Books of Lore translated by Bilbo in Rivendell.

Frodo takes the large red book and offers it, a gift, to Sam. Sam looks down at it in wonder. "Why, you have nearly finished it, Mr. Frodo!" he exclaims.

Frodo's answer is gentle, but certain: "I have quite finished, Sam," he says.

And then he adds, "The last pages are for you."

DOING WHAT THEY DID: I sit alone at my desk as I work on these last chapters. And, at the same time, I am remembering something I read in a book from another scholar, I am responding to the comments made by Linda as she marked up the rough draft of this chapter, I am imagining where you might be when your eye lights upon these stories. Sure, the word "collaboration" can be used to describe what happens when two individuals labor together start-to-finish on a single project. But collaboration also involves much larger patterns of participation, patterns that affirm the value of individual talent while at the same time recognizing how much we can benefit from the presence of others at every stage of the work that we do.

Master Samwise in His Study

Doing What the Inklings Did

 If the idea of a lonely genius working in bleak isolation is a myth, if greatness is really catalyzed by the presence of others, we should take note. And perhaps we should try to do what the Inklings did. In our own creative endeavors. In invention and technology. In business. In research, community service, and outreach.

The Inklings thrived as a group for nearly 20 years, more than twice the average timespan for groups of this kind. What do we learn from their example? What steps can we take to maximize our own efforts to connect and collaborate? Here are some suggestions:

Start Small

We often think that the way to get a group started (a small group at church, an initiative in our community, a writing group, a fan club) is to advertise widely, get a large number of people together, and then cross our fingers and hope for the best as the group whittles down to a manageable size.

Many of us have tried that. It's frustrating. It's exhausting. And most often, it just doesn't work.

The Inklings teach us the enormous power of starting small. As we saw in chapter 2, Lewis and Tolkien found that they enjoyed one another's company and shared a number of important interests. So they made a very simple decision: to meet every Monday morning for lunch and conversation. Lewis soon found it was the "pleasantest spot" in his week. And, once established, this little lunchtime grew into something really big.

Takeaway: All you need is two people, maybe three, to gather to your cause. Start a regular pattern of meeting. Define your identity. Clarify your purpose. Then invite others to join you.

Stay Focused

Of all the factors that made the Inklings successful, I think this one may be the most important. Small groups flourish when they exist for a specific purpose but begin to unravel when they attempt too many things.

The center of gravity for the Inklings was the Thursday writers group. These regular meetings focused on sharing and improving their writing. They followed a structure. They opened with a ritual: First, tea. Then pipes. Then Lewis would boom out, "Well, has nobody got anything to read us?" Manuscripts, read and critiqued, formed the center of their circle.

Other activities may flourish in widening circles alongside the good work you do. But a clear focus holds it all together.

You can't do it all. What will your defining purpose be? Forming a group of volunteers? Choose one task in the community to tackle together. Leading a church group? Choose one book or specific topic to study. Founding a writers group? Stay focused on reading and critiquing each other's work. Or decide that your writing group will not read manuscripts but gather regularly for encouragement, or prayer, or accountability. Or perhaps to sit together and problem solve, share struggles, and suggest practical solutions to help each writer stay on track.

Takeaway: Don't scatter your attention trying to jam too many priorities into your meeting time. Define your own center of gravity, and stick to it.

Meet Often

The Inklings met to read manuscripts each Thursday starting at about 9:00 p.m. That regular rhythm held them together.

But they found additional ways to stay in touch. They met again with a larger, more informal group on Tuesday mornings at The Eagle and Child pub, sitting in a small back room where, as Lewis says, the fun was "fast and furious." Throughout the week, two or three would gather for lunch or visit in one another's homes. Then they added occasional walking tours, ham suppers, and other special celebrations.

They even held impromptu Inklings meetings. In his diary entry for 15 March 1945, Warren Lewis reports, "After stopping for beer on the way home, we settled down to an Inkling *in partibus* in the lounge of the Exchange [in Liverpool]."

The Inklings ate, read, talked, worked, walked, and lived life in community. They made time for intentional meetings and spontaneous meals, focused time, and unstructured play. They made it a priority to stay in touch. Yes, we are busy, but then, so were they.

Takeaway: Establish a regular focused meeting time. Then expand and deepen the connection and keep in touch in other ways: letters, emails, phone calls, walks, and meals. Good ideas gain momentum from regular contact in a variety of settings.

Embrace Difference

Some people say the Inklings were close friends despite their differences. But that's not how it worked. The Inklings were close friends and effective collaborators *because* of their differences. They brought different skills and contrasting points of view. They trained in different disciplines and worked in different fields. As Lewis observed, "We were by no means men of one trade." And that meant there was plenty of conflict, as well as many unexpected benefits. Lewis explains it this way: "Out of this perpetual dogfight a community of mind and a deep affection emerge."

The Inklings not only lived as a diverse community, but they also made it a key concept in their fiction. In *The Lord of the Rings,* we see a fellowship of hobbits, elves, dwarves, and wizards joining forces against a common foe. In *That Hideous Strength,* Lewis creates the household of St. Anne's, which includes professors, students, housewives, gardeners, jackdaws, cats, angels, a bear, the Fisher King, and even Merlin himself. And we see it again in Charles Williams's Company of Logres, celebrated in his Arthurian poems, *Taliessin through Logres* and *The Region of the Summer Stars.*

In each case, the individuals work well together because they are different, not in spite of their differences. As Dr. Havard emphasizes, "Our differences laid the foundation of a friendship that lasted." The point is clear—Havard does not say similarities helped them overcome their many differences. He says the differences themselves were the foundation.

Takeaway: Go out of your way to cultivate a conversation with people who share your interests but see things from a very different point of view. Learn to listen generously, especially when you disagree.

Start Early and Intervene Often

One misconception about writing groups is that they exist to critique a draft-in-progress. However, many of the defining moments for the Inklings took place before a single line was written: thinking of a subject, making a wager, offering practical help. And their activity continued even after a book was published: writing a review, contributing a blurb for the cover, lending their copy to others, quoting a friend in one's own work.

How can you help others to recognize that their private hobby has the potential to reach a wider audience (the way Lewis encouraged Tolkien)? How can you use your connections to actively promote their work to a larger public (the way the Inklings promoted Charles Williams)? Become aware of these opportunities. By doing so, you will help the members of your circle and enrich the lives of others.

There is one more thing to remember. Writers and inventors who regularly collaborate often focus too narrowly on the project at hand. But remember: good collaboration takes a larger view. Reflecting on a finished project can inspire another. Comments on one book can strengthen the next. Encouragement on a successful project can help the creator to gather strength to launch into something new. From time to time, let the focus shift from nurturing the project to investing in the one who made it. Even if the book is already published, or the project is already launched, or the deal is already signed, reflecting back on what worked (and what didn't) can help the inventor and change the future.

Takeaway: It's never too early—or too late—to contribute to the success of a project.

Criticize But Don't Silence

As we saw in chapter 4, the Inklings were brutally frank. They criticized. They teased. They disliked a lot of what each other had to say. Correction is necessary. After offering some sharp advice to one aspiring writer, Lewis remarked, "I hope you don't mind me telling you all this? One can learn only by seeing one's mistakes." They believed in being frank.

Clearly, part of the secret of their success was this habit of being brutally honest. But there is a more subtle distinction to be made. It is one thing to criticize; it is quite another to dismiss someone's work altogether. Generally, the Inklings were able to make the important distinction between "I don't personally like this" and "This isn't any good."

However, one of the reasons for their dissolution is that Hugo Dyson crossed this line. When he persisted in dismissing *The Lord of the Rings,* it changed the group. Dyson didn't critique the work: he rejected it altogether. That eroded the spirit of the Inklings. It was no longer safe to share rough drafts and far-fetched ideas. When creative people encounter thoughtful critique, they feel empowered. When they encounter dismissal, they stop taking risks. They shut down.

Tolkien models this well. His initial reaction to The Chronicles of Narnia was to totally reject it. But then, over time, he realized that even though it did not appeal to him personally, others saw great value in it. He was able to recognize this and gladly recommend it.

Takeaway: Learn to tell the difference between "I don't like this" and "This doesn't have any potential."

Vary Feedback

There is an art to giving good feedback. The Inklings helped one another by making many different kinds of comments. Chapter 2 showed encouragement and pressure. Chapter 3 illustrated frank criticism and chapter 4 various kinds of editing and specific suggestions. Here are some of the different kinds of comments they offered one another as they worked together:

> Resonating: "I understand what you are trying to do."
> Praising: "This is good!"
> Encouraging: "You have what it takes."
> Pressuring: "Finish this."
> Modeling: "Look: here's what worked for me."
> Opposing: "This isn't working."
> Editing: "Try this instead."

Takeaway: Giving feedback doesn't mean telling someone what is wrong and showing them how to fix it. Giving feedback includes a whole menu of thoughtful responses. Choosing the right response at the right time is the key.

Increase the Channels

The Inklings lived near each other, and many of them worked at the same university. They found a variety of ways to communicate with each other. They met face-to-face in large groups and small ones; they also wrote long detailed critiques, short poems, and collaborative stories. Different settings favor different communication styles: structured, brief, playful, personal, public, open-ended, patient, noisy, reflective. Each format has its own advantages, and different people will tend to feel more comfortable in one mode than another. Using a variety of approaches allows more scope to express thoughts and ideas.

Technology makes it easier than ever for friends to talk and share information. Use a number of different ways (virtual and face-to-face) to stay connected.

Takeaway: Don't limit yourself to one way of exchanging ideas. Think about how you might take advantage of different forms of communication. Be inventive.

Try More Than One

The Inklings may seem like an unparalleled achievement. Warren Lewis calls their group a "famous and heroic gathering, one that has already passed into literary legend." Their legacy may seem daunting, but as we saw in chapter 8, creative circles and collaborative partnerships are very common. They don't all serve the same functions, and they don't all look the same.

Even the Inklings participated in a number of different groups. Tolkien was a founding member of The Tea Club and Barrovian Society, Apolausticks, and The Viking Club; he participated in Chequers, the Essay Club, and other groups, too. He founded The Coalbiters, and he invited Lewis to take part. Lewis loved The Coalbiters and The Inklings, but he was also part of The Cretaceous Perambulators, Beer and *Beowulf,* and The Cave. He joined the Martlets and the Mermaid Club, and he was president of both.

Takeaway: Different groups serve different purposes. You may benefit from participating in (or creating) more than one.

Think Outside the Group

The principles modeled by the Inklings and described in this book can be used to start and sustain a healthy writers group or creative cluster. They also might urge you to take much smaller steps to share your work with others.

Simply taking time to explain a project to one other person not only clarifies our own sense of the project but also opens the door to fresh perspectives. Describing how we are going about a project may inspire others by example or may invite practical suggestions or even needed resources. And the process of articulating what we are doing for another person may be what it takes for us to gain a better understanding of it for ourselves.

Look for opportunities to share your work in smaller ways. Ask for feedback on a single project. Pose a question in an online forum to solicit new ideas. Gather a few like-minded people for casual conversation over coffee. Send an email to an expert just to ask for input or bounce an idea around. Start a short-term book study. Remember the value of planting yourself in a tall forest and gather friends whose example inspires.

We need encouragement, correction, and practical suggestions. We can all use a little help from our friends.

Takeaway: Collaboration and participation take place in great groups; they also thrive when we find simple ways to include others (advisors, encouragers, even cranks and critics) at appropriate stages of the work we do.

Taking First Steps

Starting or joining a collaborative circle may sound like a giant leap, more than you are ready for. It can be overwhelming—but it is also extremely rewarding. Here are three suggestions to help you take the first steps towards expanding your view of collaboration:

1. *Read a little more.* You can learn more about the Inklings in Humphrey Carpenter's *The Inklings,* Colin Duriez's *The Oxford Inklings,* or my book *The Company They Keep.* Many authors have written about small groups, and each one comes at the topic from a different point of view. Jeff Goins talks to writers about the value of what he calls a "mastermind" group and offers practical ways to get started. Julia Cameron encourages "sacred circles" in her classic book, *The Artist's Way.* In *Organizing Genius,* Warren Bennis and Patricia Ward Biederman show how Great Groups can master the art of collaboration. Keith Sawyer promotes "collaborative webs" in *Group Genius: The Creative Power of Collaboration.* There is a lot more information (and inspiration) to explore.

2. *Consider participating online.* Internet communities make it easier than ever for people to discover others who share their interests. Sometimes, groups form online and then expand into face-to-face meetings; other times, groups meet face-to-face and then develop a larger circle of online participants. One writers group I know meets every year for a weeklong retreat, then stays in touch throughout the year through group texts and emails.

3. *Remember: two is a magic number.* A typical group has a core of 5 or 6 regulars and a larger circle of casual and occasional contributors. But as Joshua Wolf Shenk has said, more often than not the heart of the circle is a dyad, two people who are passionately interested in the same subjects and yet quite different in temperament, background, and expertise. Keep a lookout for people like this. Make it a point to make a connection.

Permissions

Permission to use excerpts from published and unpublished material has been granted by the following publishers and bodies.

Excerpts from *Brothers and Friends: The Diaries of Major Warren Hamilton Lewis* © 1982 are reprinted by the generous permission of The Marion E. Wade Center, Wheaton College, Wheaton, Illinois. All rights reserved.

Excerpts from *The Collected Letters of C. S. Lewis Volume I* © 2000 and *The Collected Letters of C. S. Lewis Volume II* © 2004, copyright C. S. Lewis Pte. Ltd., are reprinted by permission of C. S. Lewis Pte. Ltd. All rights reserved.

Excerpts from *The Lays of Beleriand* by J. R. R. Tolkien copyright © 1985 by Frank Richard Williamson and Christopher Reuel Tolkien as Executors of the Estate of J. R. R. Tolkien; and *Sauron Defeated* by J. R. R. Tolkien copyright © 1992 by Frank Richard Williamson and Christopher Reuel Tolkien as Executors of the Estate of J. R. R. Tolkien: all are reprinted by permission of Houghton Mifflin Harcourt Publishing Company. US rights. All rights reserved.

Excerpts from *The Letters of J. R. R. Tolkien*, edited by Humphrey Carpenter with the assistance of Christopher Tolkien copyright © 1981 by George Allen & Unwin (Publishers) Ltd. are reprinted by permission of Houghton Mifflin Harcourt Publishing Company. US rights. All rights reserved.

Chapter 1 is based on an article previously published in *Argentus* 2008, Issue 8, and it is adapted and reprinted here with gratitude to Steven H. Silver.

Notes

1. Dusting for Fingerprints

p. 4 "anything more to say" (Tolkien, *Letters* 24)
p. 5 "Christmas vacation" and "'hobbit talk' amuses me" (Tolkien, *Letters* 36)
p. 6 "poor ruined Hobbit!" (Tolkien, *Shadow* 49–50)
p. 6 "poor old hobbit!" (Tolkien, *Lord of the Rings* 69–70)

2. "An Unexpected Party"

p. 11 "needs a smack" (Lewis, *All My Road* 393)
p. 11 "trust a philologist" (Lewis, *Surprised* 216)
p. 12 "biting the coals" (Lewis, *They Stand* 298)
p. 12 "sickening intensity" (Lewis, *Surprised* 17)
p. 12 "passion for things Norse" (Lewis, *All My Road* 448)
p. 12 "bear cubs" (Edmonds 45)
p. 13 "an unknown author" (Lewis qtd. in Tolkien, *Lays* 151)
p. 13 "grumbles at individual lines" (Lewis qtd. in Carpenter, *Inklings* 30)
p. 14 "thought of poetry" (Barfield, *Owen Barfield* 5–6)
p. 14 "pleasantest spots" (Lewis, *Coll. Letters* II:16)
p. 14 "mythology grew up" (Lewis, *Coll. Letters* I:230–31)
p. 15 "best loved men" and "fighting a duel" (Hooper, *C. S. Lewis* 644–45)
p. 15 "thoroughgoing supernaturalist" (Lewis, *Surprised* 226)
p. 15 "hideously shocked" (Lewis, *Surprised* 206)
p. 15 "Dangers lie in wait" (Lewis, *Surprised* 226)
p. 16 "entered a monastery" (Lewis, *Coll. Letters* I:882–83)
p. 16 "reluctant convert" (Lewis, *Surprised* 228–29)

p. 16 "exhilarating" (W. H. Lewis, *Brothers* 97)

p. 16 "loves truth" (Lewis, *Coll. Letters* I:917–18)

p. 17 *"it really happened"* (Lewis, *Coll. Letters* I:976–77)

p. 17 "immediate human causes" (Lewis, *Coll. Letters* II:501)

p. 17 "thousands of soldiers" (West 82–83)

p. 17 "huddled for warmth" (Lewis, *Surprised* 19)

p. 17 "developing an affection" (Kirkpatrick qtd. in Hooper, *C. S. Lewis* 698)

p. 18 "engrossing tasks" (W. H. Lewis, *Brothers* 75)

p. 18 "a pleasantly ingenious pun" and "half-formed intimations" (Tolkien, *Letters* 388)

p. 19 "influenza" (Havard 350)

p. 19 "keenly interested" (Sayer, *Jack* 151)

p. 19 "a group of us" (Oral history Interview with R. E. Havard, conducted by Lyle W. Dorsett for the Marion E. Wade Center [26 July 1984], page 15.)

p. 19 "dropping of the matter" (Lewis, *Letters* 33–34)

p. 20 "elected himself an Inkling" (W. H. Lewis, *Brothers* 194)

p. 20 "Aberystwyth" (W. H. Lewis, *Brothers* 200)

p. 20 "disapproved of the new candidate" (Grotta 93)

p. 20 "his essence escapes them" (Wain, *Sprightly* 147)

p. 21 "a disturbing experience" (Jones 120)

p. 21 "sheer force of love" (Hopkins ii)

p. 21 "discuss poetry or theology" (Carpenter, *Inklings* 86)

p. 21–22 "major literary events" et al. (Lewis, *Coll. Letters* II:183–84)

p. 22 "inward to the bone" (Lewis, *Essays Presented* viii)

p. 22 "looks like an angel" (Lewis, *They Stand* 500–501)

p. 22 "burning with intelligence" (Lewis, *Essays Presented* ix)

p. 22 "most angelic" (Lewis, *Coll. Letters* II:652)

p. 23 "ready for it" (Lewis, *Essays Presented* x-xi)

p. 23 "their original colour" (Carpenter, *Inklings* 128)

p. 23 "decently arrive" (C. S. Lewis, *Letters* 33–34)

p. 24 "rolling off our chairs" (Havard qtd. in Hooper, *Through Joy* 89)

p. 24 "no mutual admiration society" (C. S. Lewis, *Letters* 34)

p. 24 "profuse and detailed" (Havard 351)

p. 25 "a tutorial" (Hooper, "Martlets" 40)

p. 25 "detraction, or accusations" (Tolkien, *Letters* 128)

p. 26 "no reading on Tuesday" (W. H. Lewis qtd. in Duriez and Porter 8)

p. 26 "morning sessions in a pub" (Carpenter, *Inklings* 185)

p. 26 "sustained serious discussion." (Starr 122)

p. 26 "Homer quoted" and "declaiming in Anglo-Saxon" (Dundas-Grant 371)

p. 26 "talking bawdy" (Lewis, *They Stand* 501)

p. 26 "famous and heroic" and "rarely heard equalled"(Lewis, *Letters* 33–34)

p. 26 "learned, high-hearted" (Havard 352)

p. 27 "as good as anything" (Wain, *Sprightly* 184)

p. 27 "circle of Christian friends" (Lewis, *Coll. Letters* II:363)

p. 27 "incalculable." (Lewis, *Coll. Letters* II:501)

p. 27 "Hwæt!" (Carpenter, *Inklings* 176)

p. 27 "a secret vision" (Lewis, *Four Loves* 68)

3. The Heart of the Company

p. 29 "must forgive me" (Williams, *To Michal* 242)

p. 29 *"Gone with the Wind"* (Betjeman 2)

p. 29 "hardly be better" (Williams, *To Michal* 243–44)

p. 29 "what the devil" (Lewis, *Letters* 223)

p. 30 "embarked on the impossible" (Lewis, *Coll. Letters* II:496)

p. 30 "afraid of hidden errors" (Lewis, *Coll. Letters* III:149)

p. 30 "unceasing eagerness" (Tolkien, *Letters* 362)

p. 31 "politicians or scholars" and "misfits and malcontents" (Lewis, *Reflections* 94)

p. 31 "Praise for good work" (Lewis, *Letters* 34)

p. 32 "real magic" et al. (W. H. Lewis, *Brothers* 195–204)

p. 32 "it's so *clear*" (Lewis, *Coll. Letters* II:227–28)

p. 32 "they had not *yet* happened" (Williams, *He Came Down* 5–6)

p. 32 "last Monday's address" (Williams, *To Michal* 44)

p. 33 "teaching Wisdom." (Lewis, *Coll. Letters* II:346)

p. 33 "Battle Hill" (W. H. Lewis, unpublished letter, 19 October 1937)

p. 34 "a dangerous moment" (Lewis, *Coll. Letters* II:663)

p. 34 "drips with honey" (Lewis, unpublished letter, dated circa February 1930)

p. 34 "really great poems" (Lewis, unpublished letter, dated circa Fall 1926)

p. 34 "strong and savage" (Lewis, *All My Road* 53)

p. 34 "consoled him most" (Barfield, *Owen Barfield* 106)

p. 34 "seized a postcard" (Barfield qtd. in Huttar 108)

p. 35 "loudly recommended" (Tolkien, *Letters* 34)

p. 35 "great work of literature" (Tolkien qtd. in Carpenter, *Inklings* 182)

p. 35 "good in itself" (Carpenter, *Inklings* 198)

p. 35 "most interesting essay" (Tolkien, *Letters* 109)

p. 35 "very moving" (Tolkien qtd. in Kilby, *Tolkien* 77)

p. 35 "a great book." (Tolkien qtd. in Sayer, *Jack* 197)

p. 35 "witty," "very good," and "very amusing" (Tolkien, *Letters* 71–84)

p. 35 "a vital gift" (Hadfield, *Introduction* 70)

p. 36 "twice as intelligent" (Williams, *Descent of the Dove* v)

p. 36 "found the gold" (Hopkins ii)

p. 36 "Better, Tolkien" (Tolkien, *Letters* 376)

p. 36 *"nagging"* (emphasis added, Lewis, *Coll. Letters* III:1458)

p. 36 "a procrastinator & a perfectionist" (Lewis, "Letter to Edmund R. Meškys" 23)

p. 36 "really *good*" (Lewis, *Coll. Letters* II:96)

p. 37 "a new story" (Tolkien, *Letters* 27)

p. 37 "getting quite out of hand." (Tolkien, *Letters* 40)

p. 37 "Tolkien was discouraged" (Tolkien, *Treason* 1)

p. 37 "did not know how to go on" (Tolkien, *Letters* 321)

p. 37 "hoped to finish" (Tolkien, *Letters* 58)

p. 37 "not a line" (Tolkien, *Letters* 86)

p. 37 "*dead stuck*" (Tolkien, *Letters* 321)

p. 37 "indefatigable man" et al. (Tolkien, *Letters* 68–70)

p. 38 "never have finished" (Shippey, *Beyond*)

p. 38 "due to the encouragement" (Carpenter, *Souvenir Booklet*)

p. 38 "bandersnatch" (Lewis, *Coll. Letters* III:1049)

p. 38 "the encouragement of C. S. L." (Tolkien, *Letters* 366)

p. 38 "Only by his support" (Tolkien, *Letters* 184)

p. 38 "in spite of obstacles" (Tolkien, *Letters* 303)

p. 39 "write some ourselves" (Lewis qtd. in Tolkien, *Letters* 378)

p. 39 "an excursionary 'Thriller'" (Tolkien, *Letters* 29)

p. 39 "Atlantis legend" (Tolkien, *Letters* 378)

p. 39 "The Lost Road" and "Númenor" (Tolkien, *Lost Road* 9)

p. 40 "labour was not wasted." (Tolkien, *Letters* 209)

p. 40 "let it be supernatural" (Williams, *To Michal* 73)

p. 40 "impulse to write a play" (Barfield, *Orpheus* 7)

p. 41 "tears to my eyes" (Lewis, *Coll. Letters* II:223)

p. 41 "dozed off again" (Dundas-Grant 372)

p. 42 "The Lewis Papers" (W. H. Lewis, unpublished letter, 22 Oct 1968)

p. 42 "do not see any danger" (W. H. Lewis, *Brothers* 147)

p. 42 "It's catching!" (Tolkien, *Letters* 71)

p. 42 "an historian" (Morgan 383)

p. 42 "wit and good sense" (Carpenter, *Inklings* 243)

p. 43 "not so bad" (W. H. Lewis, *Brothers* 300)

p. 43 "Jack could knock down" (Barfield, *Owen Barfield* 127)

p. 44 "opening of a flower" (Knight 295)

p. 44 "good in quite another way" (Tolkien, *Letters* 366)

p. 44 "not even trying" (Lewis, *Letters* 430)

p. 45 "The covered bath" (Hadfield, *Charles Williams* 179)

p. 45 "see my refuge" (Williams, *To Michal* 18)

p. 45 "follies, and *scares*" (W. H. Lewis, *Brothers* 265)

p. 46 "this interesting belief" (Wheeler 48–49)

p. 46 "give it back" and "get it out of him" (Lewis, *Coll. Letters* II:198–99)

p. 47 "CSL's *Allegory of Love*" (Williams, *Letters to Lalage* 66)

p. 47 "read *Sir Gawain*" (Lewis, *Letters* 285)

p. 47 "*good* characters" (Lewis, *Letters* 322)

p. 47 "warned and enlightened" (Williams, "Rev. of *Screwtape*" 170)

p. 47 "Snigsozzle" (Williams, "Letters in Hell" 245–46)

p. 47 "goodness working on goodness" (Williams, "Rev. of *Problem of Pain*" 62)

p. 48 "obviously knows" and "so ripe, so friendly" (Lewis, "*Hobbit*" 81–82)

p. 48 "nose for an elf" (Lewis, "Professor Tolkien's" 20)

p. 48 "prove a classic" (Lewis, "*Hobbit*" 82)

p. 48 "break your heart," et al. (Lewis, "Tolkien's *Lord of the Rings*" 84–90)

p. 48 "Boramir" Lewis was a notoriously bad speller, especially when he attempted to write down the name of a character from a story he had only heard read aloud. His misspelling of "Boromir" here is an example.

p. 49 "its blaze" (Lewis, "Sacred" 268)

p. 49 "for Christmas presents" (C. Tolkien, Foreword *Hobbit* n. pag.)

4. "I've a good mind to punch your head."

p. 53 "hungry for rational opposition" (see, for example, Tillyard and Lewis 41)

p. 53 "brutally frank" (Lewis, *Letters* 34)

p. 53 "criticism was free." (Oral History Interview with R. E. Havard, conducted by Lyle W. Dorsett for the Marion E. Wade Center [26 July 1984], page 16)

p. 53 "dialectical swordplay" (Lewis, *Letters* 34)

p. 53 "a bit aggressive" (Barfield, *Owen Barfield* 127)

p. 53 "a peashooter against a howitzer" (Barfield, *Owen Barfield* 28)

p. 54 "rough academic arena" (Tillyard and Lewis 69)

p. 54 "punch your head" (Lewis, *Coll. Letters* II:228)

p. 54 "drawing their guns" (Tolkien, *Letters* 103)

p. 54 "eminently combustible" (Lewis, *Coll. Letters* II:283)

p. 55 "obscurity beyond belief" (Havard 351)

p. 55 "clotted glory from Charles" (Dyson qtd. in Lewis, *Coll. Letters* II:501)

p. 55 "make head or tail of it" (Auden ix-x)

p. 55 "mere butter bath!" (Lewis, *Coll. Letters* II:186–87)

p. 55 "for all I was worth." (emphasis added, Lewis, *Coll. Letters* II:819)

p. 56 "good for my mind." (Williams, *To Michal* 89)

p. 56 "*like a dogfight*" (emphasis added, Lewis, *Letters* 179)

p. 56 "dogmatic pronouncements" (Tolkien, *Letters* 103)

p. 56 "man who disagrees" (Lewis, *Surprised* 199)

p. 56 "incessant disputation" (Lewis, *Surprised* 207)

p. 57 "how to think" (Barfield, *Owen Barfield* 9)

p. 57 "weakest portions" (Adey 13)

p. 57 "Opposition is true friendship." (Barfield, Dedication, *Poetic Diction* n. pag.)

p. 57 "wake scared and unrefreshed" et al. (Williams, *To Michal* 163–71)

p. 59 "mainly due to C. S. L." (Tolkien, *Letters* 349)

p. 59 "Well, I'm back." (Tolkien, *Lord of the Rings* 1008)

p. 59–60 "the text continued" et al. The epilogue to *The Lord of the Rings* and Christopher Tolkien's commentary on it are found in *Sauron Defeated* pages 114–35.

p. 60 "One must stop somewhere." (Tolkien, *Letters* 179)

p. 60 "destroyed the ending" (Tolkien, *Letters* 227)

p. 61 "point about Virgil" and "gross understatement" (W. H. Lewis, *Brothers* 198)

p. 61 "the nothingness of the utterness" (W. H. Lewis, *Brothers* 257)

p. 62 "appropriate for an essay" (Barfield, *Owen Barfield* 37)

p. 62 "your ugly face" (Lewis, *Coll. Letters* II:574–75)

p. 62 "*polyvalence* instead of *multivalence?*" (Lewis, *Coll. Letters* III:1328)

p. 62 "answering the question" (W. H. Lewis, unpublished letter, 2 July 1970)

p. 62–63 "far above his head" and "far too abstruse" (W. H. Lewis, *Brothers* 273–75)

p. 63 "limited sympathies" (Tolkien, *Letters* 349)

p. 63 "My taste is not normal." (Tolkien, *Letters* 34)

p. 63 "confusion of thought" (Tolkien, *Letters* 60)

p. 63 "new moral allegory" (Tolkien, *Letters* 71)

p. 63 "wherever I smell it" (Tolkien in a BBC interview, posted at http://daisy.freeserve.co.uk/jrrt_int.htm and accessed 20 May 2005.)

p. 63 "a fixed manner" (Tolkien, *Letters* 302)

p. 63 "would not be publishable." (Tolkien, *Letters* 352)

p. 63 "to the public" (Dorsett, *Seeking* 58)

p. 64 "not a popular evangelist!" (Rogers 54)

p. 64 "animosity C. S. L. seems to excite" (Tolkien, *Letters* 184)

p. 64 "religious nature" (Tolkien qtd. in Hooper, *Through Joy* 125)

p. 64 "I'm hated" (Lewis qtd. in Mitchell, "Bearing" 7)

p. 64 "scholarly claim to the appointments." (Mitchell, "Bearing" 8)

p. 65 "as bad as can be" (Tolkien qtd. in Sayer, "Recollections" 25)

p. 65 "Doesn't he know what he's talking about?" (Tolkien qtd. in Green and Hooper 241)

p. 65 "almost worthless" (Sayer, *Jack* 189)

p. 65 "disliked it intensely" et al. (Green and Hooper 241)

p. 65 "single imaginative country" (Graham 156)

p. 65–66 "mythological terms" and "a child's story" (Christopher, "Narnian" 41)

p. 66 "His use of 'Numinor'" (Carpenter, *Tolkien* 174)

p. 66 "mere jealousy" (Tolkien, *Letters* 127)

p. 67 "did not interfere" (Unpublished letter from Tolkien to Eileen Elgar, dated 24 December 1971 [private collection], qtd. in Long 39)

p. 67 "dislike allegory" (Tolkien, *Fellowship* xv)

p. 67 "My mind does not work allegorically." (Tolkien, *Letters* 174)

p. 67 "entirely foreign" (Tolkien, *Letters* 307)

p. 67 "the evidence is rather against Tolkien" (Shippey, *J. R. R. Tolkien* 161)

p. 67 "urged her to read them" and "indifferent to Narnia"(Long 39–40)

p. 67 "outside the range of my sympathy" (Tolkien, *Letters* 352)

p. 68 "not inflict them on us" and "no picture of human life" (Wain, "John Wain" 329)

p. 68 "can't get through it." (Oral History Interview with Stella Aldwinckle, conducted by Lyle W. Dorsett for the Marion E. Wade Center [26 July 1985], page 45. Aldwinckle is describing a conversation with Owen Barfield.)

p. 68 "hard to take" (Havard 352)

p. 69 "didn't like *The Lord of the Rings*" (Bratman 28)

p. 69 "felt a marked antipathy" (Wilson 216)

p. 69 "the anti-resonator" (Joe R. Christopher, personal correspondence)

p. 69 "a kind of 'veto'" (W. H. Lewis, *Brothers* 200)

p. 69 "a bit like that" (C. Tolkien, qtd. in "A Film Portrait")

p. 69 "calls it unfair" (W. H. Lewis, *Brothers,* 200)

5. "Drat That Omnibus!"

p. 74 "translation of Beowulf" (Lewis, *Coll. Letters* I:741)

p. 74 "textual indeterminancy" (Gere 75)

p. 74 "largely unintelligible fragments" (Tolkien, *Letters* 209)

p. 75 "18 different drafts" (http://www.marquette.edu/library, accessed 5 Sept. 2004)

p. 75 "over seven feet high" (Kilby, *Tolkien* 12)

p. 75 "in 'phases'" (Tolkien, *Shadow* 3)

p. 75 "chop and change" (Tolkien, *Shadow* 35)

p. 75 "laboriously pondered" (Tolkien, *Letters* 160)

p. 75 "largely re-written backwards" (Tolkien, *Fellowship* xiv)

p. 75 "complex directions" (Tolkien, *Shadow* 133)

p. 76 "world it portrays" (emphasis added, C. Tolkien, *Silmarillion* 7)

p. 76 "never satisfied" (Lewis, *Coll. Letters* II:631)

p. 77 "without a destination." (Tolkien, *Shadow* 27)

p. 77 "The Hobbit sequel" and "anything new" (Tolkien, *Letters* 29)

p. 77 "It has lost my favour" et al. (Tolkien, *Letters* 38)

p. 77 "a white horse" (Tolkien, *Shadow* 47–48)

p. 78 "a black horse" (Tolkien, *Lord of the Rings* 73–74)

p. 79 "quite unforeseen goals" (Tolkien, *Letters* 40)

p. 79 "the new Hobbit" (Tolkien, *Letters* 40)

p. 79 "*with that gravity* " (emphasis added, Lewis qtd. in Kilby, *Tolkien* 76)

p. 79 "occupies the mind" (Tolkien, *Letters* 26)

p. 79 "Elvish tongues" (Tolkien, *Letters* 247)

p. 79 "endlessly interesting" (Kilby, *Tolkien* 26)

p. 80 "more Elvish" (Tolkien, *Letters* 216)

p. 80 "great depths within himself" (Knight 5)

p. 80 "never heard of the Inklings" (Carpenter, *Inklings* 160)

p. 80 "Crack my timbers" (Tolkien, *Treason* 419)

p. 81 "dare to come round" et al. (Tolkien, *Shadow* 290–99)

p. 82 "twopenny pad" et al. (Williams and Lewis, *Arthurian* 2–23)

p. 83–87 The rough draft and revised versions of Tolkien's *The Lay of Leithian* are found in *The Lays of Beleriand,* pages 150–308. Lewis's comments on *The Lay of Leithian* are found in *The Lays of Beleriand,* pages 315–29.

p. 87–89 All of Tolkien's comments on the Saruman passage can be found in his response to Charlotte and Denis Plimmer, published in Tolkien's *Letters,* pages 372–78. The rough draft of the passage is found in Tolkien's *War of the Ring,* pages 30–67. The final version of the passage is published in *The Lord of the Rings,* pages 563–70.

p. 88 "dead stuck" (Tolkien, *Letters* 321)

p. 90 "a man revising" (Hooper qtd. in Phillips 113)

p. 90 *"Dymer,* for example" (Hooper, *C. S. Lewis* 145–47)

p. 91 "one word less wd. make all the difference." (Lewis, *They Stand* 446)

p. 91 "exercise your textual criticism" (Lewis, *Coll. Letters* II:527)

p. 91–92 "Drat that Omnibus!" et al. (Hooper, *C. S. Lewis* 103)

p. 92 "a few days" (Harwood 377)

p. 92 "change there" and "appeared in print" (Lewis, *Poems* vii–viii)

p. 92 "akin to parturition" (Havard 358)

p. 92–93 "hundreds of conversations" and "begin all over" (Morris 319–26)

p. 93 "immediate problem" and "What's a chap to do?" (Lewis, *Letters* 424)

p. 93 "listen to what I said" (Gresham 2)

p. 94 "add a caution" (Lewis, *Coll. Letters* II:942–43)

p. 94 "her face" and "very foolish" (Lewis, *Lion* 7)

p. 94 "not a magic one" (Lewis, *Lion* 27)

p. 95 "One listener complained" (Lewis, *Mere Christianity* 31)

p. 95 "a good many people" (Lewis, *Mere Christianity* 157)

p. 95 "going to tell you" (Lewis, *Mere Christianity* 119)

p. 95 "his own barriers" and "elusive and incalculable" (Lewis, *Essays Presented* x)

p. 96 "Lewis's strengths and weaknesses" (Downing, *Planets* 35)

p. 96–97 "enthralling" et al. (Tolkien, *Letters* 32–33)

p. 97 "mere fiction" et al. (Lewis, *Out of the Silent Planet* 156–60)

p. 98 "life-long critic" (Lewis, Dedication, *Out of the Silent Planet* n. pag.)

p. 98 "time-travelling as well" (Lewis, *Out of the Silent Planet* 160)

p. 99 "thoughtful comments and practical suggestions" (Barfield, Foreword *Saving* n. pag.)

p. 99 "patience in listening" (W. H. Lewis, *Sunset* x)

p. 99 "corrections and suggestions" (Bennett, *Parlement* v)

p. 99 "advice and criticism." (Lewis, *English Literature* vii)

p. 99 "minor problems" (Mathew, *Court of Richard II* xi)

p. 99 "frequent personal guidance" (Wrenn, *A Study* vi)

p. 99 "my approach to *Beowulf*" (Wrenn, *Beowulf* 5)

p. 99 "suggestions they have made" (Coghill, *Poet Chaucer* viii)

p. 100 "hard-hitting criticism" (Lewis, *Essays Presented* v)

6. Mystical Caboodle

p. 104 "less like a house" (Lewis, *Surprised* 9–10)

p. 104 "little end room" (Lewis, *Coll. Letters* I:107)

p. 104 "every color" (Lewis, *Surprised* 14)

p. 105 "borrow from his friends" (Christopher, *C. S. Lewis* 2)

p. 105 "social life of the college" et al. (Baker 65–67)

p. 106 "produces the fun" and "round-robin story-telling" (Lewis, *Coll. Letters* II:384–85)

p. 106 "magically changed" (Lewis, *Coll. Letters* I:689–90)

p. 106 "Longus" (Barfield and Lewis, *Cretaceous* n. pag.)

p. 106 "glorious country" (Lewis, *Coll. Letters* I:690)

p. 107 "in the metre of Hiawatha." (Lewis, *They Stand* 352)

p. 107 "mystical caboodle" (Barfield and Lewis, *Cretaceous* n. pag.)

p. 107 "Button Moulder's story" (Lewis, *All My Road* 60)

p. 107 "The Glass House" et al. (Green and Hooper 274)

p. 108 "A is the Absolute" (Barfield and Lewis, "Abecedarium" 298)

p. 109 "the best map reader" (Barfield and Lewis, *Cretaceous* n. pag.)

p. 109 "Soaking-Machine" (Lewis, *Coll. Letters* I:119)

p. 109 "Jack smoked a cigarette." (Sayer, *Jack* 207)

p. 110 "a peculiarly Oxonian character" (Tennyson xvi)

p. 111 "Language (Nature, Origins, Functions)" (Lewis, *Letters* 105)

p. 111 "in the blueprint stage" (Walsh 10)

p. 111 "SCRAPS" (Beebe 9)

p. 111 "Greek Kalends" (Lewis, *Coll. Letters* III:6)

p. 111 "a short Xtian Dictionary" (Lewis, *Coll. Letters* II:721–22)

p. 112 "a book of animal stories" (*Lewis, Essays Presented* xii)

p. 112 "my own principles" (Lewis, *Problem* 9)

p. 112 "offered many suggestions" (Sayer, *Jack* 162)

p. 112 "effects of pain" (Lewis, *Problem* 143)

p. 112 "get it right" (Havard 356–57)

p. 113 "took the initiative" (Lewis, *Coll. Letters* II:649)

p. 113 "offer as a memorial" (Lewis, *Essays Presented* vi)

p. 113 "corporate identity" (Carpenter, *Inklings* 224)

p. 114 "imperfectly, yet usefully" (Williams and Lewis 1–2)

p. 114 "technique is very different" (Mathew, "Williams and the Arthuriad" 14)

p. 114 *"permanent member"* (Tolkien qtd. in Carpenter, *Inklings* 205)

p. 115 "chief critic and collaborator" (Tolkien, *Letters* 118)

p. 115 "In a hole in the ground" (C. Tolkien, Foreword *Hobbit* n. pag.)

p. 115 "consistency of the story" (John Tolkien and Priscilla Tolkien, *Family Album* 58)

p. 115 "strode across the room" (C. Tolkien, Foreword *Hobbit* n. pag.)

p. 115 "paid him twopence" (Tolkien, *Letters* 28)

p. 115 "discussing the ideas" (John Tolkien and Priscilla Tolkien 73)

p. 115 "your opinion matters" (Tolkien, *Letters* 91)

p. 116 "made a better job of it" (Carpenter, *Inklings* 205)

p. 116 "started with a map" (Tolkien, *Letters* 177)

p. 116 "never make a map" (*J. R. R. Tolkien: An Audio*)

p. 116 "meticulous care for distances" (Tolkien, *Letters* 177)

p. 116 "My heart and mind is in the *Silmarillion*" (Tolkien, *Letters* 261)

p. 117 "his invented peoples" (Cater 91)

p. 117–19 "labyrinth of story" et al. (C. Tolkien, *Silmarillion: A Brief Account* n. pag.)

p. 117 "personal literary judgment" (C. Tolkien qtd. in Cater 94)

p. 118 "remained unpublished" and "his latest intention"(C. Tolkien, *Sir Gawain* 7–8)

p. 119 "the benefit of two lifetimes' work" (Unwin 6)

p. 119 "collective action stage" (Farrell 286)

p. 120 "Well, we will." (Lewis qtd. in Fox 187)

p. 120 *"practising poets"* (Tolkien, *Letters* 36)

p. 120 "demonstrate their power" (Carpenter, *Inklings* 163)

p. 120 "a final vote of 173 to 194" (Hooper, *C. S. Lewis* 56)

p. 120 "written *The Screwtape Letters*" and "'merry' despite the defeat" (W. H. Lewis, *Brothers* 239–40)

p. 121 "my friends seem to be upset" (Lewis, *Letters* 351)

p. 121 "Lewis was chosen unanimously" et al. (Hooper, *C. S. Lewis* 68)

p. 121 "You will not find the warrior" (Lewis, *Four Loves* 71)

7. Faces in a Mirror

p. 125 "talking of dragons" (Lewis, *Rehabilitations* 122)

p. 126 "Chaucerian verse" (Lewis, *Selected Literary Essays* x). Here's a rough translation: "In Oxford, some accomplished students gathered in a good company. I was one, and you will note that the group was worthy and wise. Sir Lewis was there, a good philosopher. He offered us a noble paper. He spoke Greek very well, and yet, he looked very young."

p. 126 "lives at Magdalen College" (Barfield, Epigraph, *Owen Barfield* n. pag.)

p. 127 "Biographia Theologia" (Barfield qtd. in Glyer 177)

p. 128 "clerihews." All of Tolkien's clerihews are quoted from Carpenter's, *Inklings*, pages 177–87.

p. 128 "classical antiquity" (Freeman-Grenville ix–x)

p. 129 "J. R. R. T. for C. S. L." (Tolkien, *Tree* 7)

p. 129 *"really happened"* (Lewis, *Coll. Letters* I:977)

p. 130 "man, sub-creator" et al. The final version of the poem "Mythopoeia" is published in Tolkien's *Tree and Leaf,* pages 97–101.

p. 130 "Not easily it flows" et al. Tolkien's poem about Charles Williams is untitled. It has been printed in its entirety in Carpenter's *Inklings*, pages 123–26.

p. 132 "not so agile" et al. (Lewis, *Boxen* 69)

p. 132 "much in common" (Lewis, *Surprised* 81)

p. 132 "through the mazes" (Downing, *"Editor's Introduction"* xvii–xviii)

p. 133 "Mr. Bultitude the bear" (Lewis, *Coll. Letters* II:682)

p. 133 "booming voice" (Carpenter, *Tolkien* 194)

p. 133 "I do not travel" (Tolkien, *Letters* 288–89)

p. 134 "a short story in his head" (Carpenter, *Tolkien* 196)

p. 134 "a country began to open out" (Tolkien, *Tree* 75–76)

p. 134 "bedroom window" (Tolkien, *Tree* 6)

p. 134 "mythological Tree" (Carpenter, *Tolkien* 196)

p. 135 "Ælfwine" (Tolkien, *Lost Road* 37–38)

p. 135 "based on her father" (Tolkien, *Letters* 89)

p. 135 "Martian language and culture" (Glover 77)

p. 135 "intelligentsia on a holiday." (Lewis, *Out of the Silent Planet* 7)

p. 135 "neatly dressed" (Kilby, *Tolkien* 24)

p. 136 "a thin cold rain" (Lewis, *Coll. Letters* I:757)

p. 136 "fond of water" et al. (Downing, *Planets* 102–200)

p. 136 "great vigour" (emphasis added, Carpenter, *Inklings* 198)

p. 136 "but not of me" (Lewis, "Reply to Professor Haldane" 73)

p. 136 "a man called B." (Lewis, *Perelandra* 32)

p. 137 "influential theories" (Lewis, *That Hideous Strength* 261)

p. 137 "the very man" (Lewis, *Perelandra* 28)

p. 137–40 "no more than a *jeu d'esprit*" et al. Tolkien's tale of the Notion Club is published in *Sauron Defeated,* pages 148–281.

p. 140 *The House of the Octopus* is published in Charles Williams's *Collected Plays.* It is an obscure work, set on a Pacific island during an invasion by the Satanic empire of P'o-l'u.

p. 141 "the great English poet" (Lewis, "Charles Walter" 265)

p. 141 "It's a larger world" (Lewis, *Collected Poems* 119)

p. 141 "a formative influence" (Lewis and Sayers 9)

p. 142 "Lewis's greatest literary achievement" (Barfield, "Clive," *Royal Society* 22)

p. 142 "a distinguished niche" (Barfield, "Clive," *Oxford Magazine* 155)

p. 142 "well hidden as a crab's" et al. (Wain, "Great Clerke" 155–60)

p. 143 "a 'magnanimous' man" (Havard 363)

p. 143 "He semeth elvyssh" et al. (Coghill, "John Ronald" 30–31)

p. 145 "essential to the final outcome" (Becker 25)

8. Leaf-Mould and Memories

p. 148 "lone-genius idea" (Shenk xvi)

p. 148 "entrepreneurial enterprise" (Wallace qtd. in Bennis and Biederman 5)

p. 149 "sixteenth-century Florence" (Shenk xvi)

p. 150 "bigotry and folly" (Williams, *Place of the Lion* 187)

p. 150 "win-win relationship" (Komisar qtd. in Simmons and accessed 20 Feb. 2015)

p. 151 "individual initiative" (LeFevre 124)

p. 151 "No one ever influenced Tolkien" (Lewis, *Coll. Letters* III:1049)

p. 152 "all the achievements" (Goethe qtd. in Bloom 52)

p. 153 "pass on the torch" (Sayers, *Further Papers* v)

p. 153 "you enter a parlor" (Burke, *Philosophy of Literary Form* 110–11)

p. 154 "across an expanse" (Shenk 13)

p. 154 "make our best work" (Shenk xxv)

p. 154 "Spin something" (Lewis, *Discarded* 211)

p. 154 "descending into the deeps" (emphasis added, Tolkien qtd. in Carpenter, *Tolkien* 126)

p. 155 "a 'leaf-mould' of memories" (Tolkien, *Letters* 409)

p. 155 "intricately knotted" et al. (Tolkien, "On Fairy-Stories" 22–28).

p. 156 "being *made possible*" (emphasis added, LeFevre 65)

p. 157 "the whole cosmos" (R. King 18)

p. 157 "all have eternal life" (Howard 11–12)

p. 157 "our common life" (*Book of Common Prayer* 34)

p. 158 "*The Red Book of Westmarch*" et al. (Tolkien, *Shadow* 1003–4)

p. 158 "There and Back Again" (Tolkien, *Hobbit* 316)

p. 158 "his friends' recollections" (Tyler 486)

p. 159 "translated by Bilbo" and "The last pages are for you." (Tolkien, *Shadow* 1004)

Epilogue

p. 162 "pleasantest spot" (Lewis, *Coll. Letters* II:16)

p. 162 "anything to read us?" (Lewis, *Letters* 13)

p. 163 "perpetual dogfight" (Lewis, *Surprised* 200)
p. 164 "Our differences laid the foundation" (Havard 350)
p. 165 "I hope you don't mind" (Lewis, *Coll. Letters* III:971)
p. 167 "famous and heroic gathering" (Lewis, *Letters* 13)

Bibliography

Adey, Lionel. *C. S. Lewis's "Great War" with Owen Barfield*. ELS Monograph Series 14. Victoria, B.C.: University of Victoria, 1978.

Auden, W. H. Introduction. *The Descent of the Dove*. By Charles Williams. New York: Meridian Books, 1956. v–xii.

Baker, Leo. "Near the Beginning." Como. 65–75.

Barfield, Owen. "Clive Staples Lewis." Obituary. *Oxford Magazine* 30 Jan. 1964: 155–56.

———. "Clive Staples Lewis." Obituary. *Report of the Royal Society of Literature* 1964: 20–22.

———. *Orpheus: A Poetic Drama*. Ed., and Afterword John C. Ulreich, Jr. West Stockbridge, MA: Lindisfarne Press, 1983.

———. *Owen Barfield on C. S. Lewis*. Ed. and Intr. G. B. Tennyson. Middletown, CT: Wesleyan University Press, 1989.

———. *Poetic Diction: A Study in Meaning*. 1928. 2nd ed. Middletown, CT: Wesleyan University Press, 1984.

———. *Saving the Appearances: A Study in Idolatry*. 1957. New York: Harvest-HBJ Book-Harcourt Brace Jovanovich, 1957.

———. *The Silver Trumpet*. 1925. Ed. Marjorie L. Mead. Longmont, CO: Bookmakers Guild, 1986.

———. *Worlds Apart*. Middletown, CT: Wesleyan University Press, 1963.

Barfield, Owen, and C. S. Lewis. "Abecedarium Philosophicum." *Oxford Magazine* 30 Nov. 1933: 298.

———. *A Cretaceous Perambulator (The Re-examination of)*. Ed. Walter Hooper. Oxford: Oxford University C. S. Lewis Society, 1983.

———. *The "Great War" of Owen Barfield and C. S. Lewis: Philosophical Writings 1927–1930*. Ed Norber Feinendegen and Arend Smilde. *Inklings Studies Supplement*. No. 1. 2015.

Becker, Howard S. *Art Worlds*. Berkeley: University of California Press, 1982.

Beebe, Steven A. "C. S. Lewis on Language and Meaning: Manuscript Fragment Identified." *Seven: An Anglo-American Literary Review*. 27. 2014: 7–24.

Bennett, J. A. W., ed. and Preface. *Essays on Malory*. 1963. Oxford: Clarendon Press, 1965. v–vii.

———. *The Parlement of Foules: An Interpretation*. Oxford: Clarendon Press, 1957.

Bennis, Warren, and Patricia Ward Biederman. *Organizing Genius: The Secrets of Creative Collaboration*. Cambridge: Perseus Books, 1997.

Betjeman, John. Rev. of *All Hallows' Eve* by Charles Williams. *Daily Herald* [London] 31 Jan 1945: 2.

Bevan, Edwyn. *Symbolism and Belief*. London: Allen & Unwin, Ltd., 1938.

Bloom, Harold. *The Anxiety of Influence: A Theory of Poetry*. London: Oxford University Press, 1975.

The Book of Common Prayer. 1928. Oxford: Oxford University Press, 2001.

Bratman, David. "Hugo Dyson: Inkling, Teacher, Bon Vivant." *Mythlore* 21.4 (whole no. 82, Winter 1997): 19–34.

Burke, Kenneth. *The Philosophy of Literary Form*. Rev. ed. New York: Vintage Books, 1957.

Cameron, Julia. *The Artist's Way: A Spiritual Path to Higher Creativity*. 1992. Los Angeles: J. P. Tarcher/Putnam, 2002.

Carpenter, Humphrey. *The Inklings: C. S. Lewis, J. R. R. Tolkien, Charles Williams, and Their Friends*. Boston: Houghton Mifflin, 1979.

———. *The Lord of the Rings: Souvenir Booklet Commemorating Twenty Five Years of Its Publication*. N. p. Allen & Unwin, 1980.

———. *Tolkien: A Biography*. Boston: Houghton Mifflin, 1977.

Carroll, Lewis. *Through the Looking-Glass and What Alice Found There*. 1871. Oxford: Oxford University Press, 1982.

Cater, William. "The Filial Duty of Christopher Tolkien." *The Tolkien Scrapbook*. Ed. Alida Becker. Philadelphia: Running Press, 1978. 90–95.

Cecil, David. *Two Quiet Lives: Dorothy Osborne, Thomas Gray*. Indianapolis, IN: Bobbs-Merrill, 1948.

Christopher, Joe R. *C. S. Lewis*. Twayne's English Authors Series. Boston: Twayne, 1987.

———. "J. R. R. Tolkien, Narnian Exile." *Mythlore* 15.1 (whole no. 55, Autumn 1988): 37–45; 15.2 (whole no. 56, Winter 1988): 17–23.

Coghill, Nevill, trans. *The Canterbury Tales*. By Geoffrey Chaucer. Baltimore: Penguin, 1952.

———. *The Collected Papers of Nevill Coghill, Shakespearian and Medievalist*. Ed. and Introduction Douglas Gray. Sussex: Harvester Press, 1988.

———. "John Ronald Reuel Tolkien." Obituary. *Report of the Royal Society of Literature*. 1973–74 and 1974–75: 30–33.

———. *The Poet Chaucer*. 1949. 2nd ed. London: Oxford University Press, 1967.

Coghill, Nevill, and Christopher Tolkien, eds. *Chaucer: The Man of Law's Tale*. Harrap's English Classics. London: Harrap, 1969.

———, eds. *Chaucer: The Nun's Priest's Tale*. 1959. Harrap's English Classics. London: Harrap, 1977.

———, eds. *Chaucer: The Pardoner's Tale*. 1958. Harrap's English Classics. London: Harrap, 1980.

Como, James, ed. *Remembering C. S. Lewis: Recollections of Those Who Knew Him*. San Francisco: Ignatius Press, 2005. Rpt. of *C. S. Lewis at the Breakfast Table and Other Reminiscences*. 1979.

Davis, Norman, and C. L. Wrenn, eds. *English and Medieval Studies Presented to J. R. R. Tolkien on the Occasion of His Seventieth Birthday*. London: Allen & Unwin, 1962.

Dorsett, Lyle. *Seeking the Secret Place: The Spiritual Formation of C. S. Lewis*. Grand Rapids, MI: Brazos Press, 2004.

Downing, David C. "Editor's Introduction." *The Pilgrim's Regress* by C. S. Lewis. Wade Annotated Edition. Grand Rapids, MI: Eerdmans, 2014.

———. *Planets in Peril: A Critical Study of C. S. Lewis's Ransom Trilogy*. Amherst: University of Massachusetts Press, 1992.

Dundas-Grant, James. "From an 'Outsider.'" Como 368–74.

Duriez, Colin. *The Oxford Inklings: Lewis, Tolkien and their Circle*. Oxford: Lion Books, 2015.

Duriez, Colin, and David Porter. *The Inklings Handbook: A Comprehensive Guide to the Lives, Thought and Writings of C. S. Lewis, J. R. R. Tolkien, Charles Williams, Owen Barfield and their Friends*. St. Louis: Chalice Press, 2001.

Dyson, H. V. D., and John Butt. *Augustans and Romantics: 1689–1830*. Introductions to English Literature 3. London: Cresset Press, 1961.

Edmonds, E. L. "C. S. Lewis, the Teacher." *In Search of C. S. Lewis*. Ed. Stephen Schofield. South Plainfield, NJ: Bridge, 1983. 37–51.

Farrell, Michael P. *Collaborative Circles: Friendship Dynamics and Creative Work*. Chicago: University of Chicago Press, 2001.

A Film Portrait of J. R. R. Tolkien. Dir. Derek Bailey. Narr. Judi Dench. Visual Corporation, 1992.

Flieger, Verlyn, and Carl F. Hostetter, eds. *Tolkien's Legendarium: Essays on The History of Middle-earth*. Contributions to the Study of Science Fiction and Fantasy 86. Westport, CT: Greenwood Press, 2000.

Fox, Adam. "At the Breakfast Table." Como 179–88.

Freeman-Grenville, G. S. P. "The Rev. Fr. Gervase Mathew." *Azania: Archaeological Research in Africa* 11 (1976): ix–x.

Gere, Anne Ruggles. *Writing Groups: History, Theory, and Implications*. Carbondale: Southern Illinois University Press, 1987.

Glover, Donald E. *C. S. Lewis: The Art of Enchantment*. Athens: Ohio University Press, 1981.

Glyer, Diana Pavlac. *The Company They Keep: C. S. Lewis and J. R. R. Tolkien as Writers in Community.* Kent, OH: Kent State University Press, 2007.

Graham, David, ed. *We Remember C. S. Lewis: Essays and Memoirs.* Nashville, TN: Broadman and Holman, 2001.

Green, Roger Lancelyn, and Walter Hooper. *C. S. Lewis: A Biography.* San Diego: Harcourt Brace, 1974.

Gresham, Douglas H. Foreword. *Letters to Children.* By C. S. Lewis. Ed. Lyle W. Dorsett and Marjorie Lamp Mead. New York: Collier-Macmillan, 1985. 1–2.

Grotta, Daniel. *J. R. R. Tolkien: Architect of Middle Earth.* Philadelphia: Running Press, 1992.

Hadfield, Alice Mary. *Charles Williams: An Exploration of His Life and Work.* New York: Oxford University Press, 1983.

———. *An Introduction to Charles Williams.* London: Robert Hale, 1959.

Harwood, A. C. "A Toast to His Memory." Como 377–82.

Havard, R. E. "Philia: Jack at Ease." Como 349–67.

Hooper, Walter. *C. S. Lewis: A Companion and Guide.* New York: HarperSanFrancisco, 1996.

———. *Through Joy and Beyond: A Pictorial Biography of C. S. Lewis.* New York: Macmillan, 1982.

———. "To the Martlets." *C. S. Lewis: Speaker and Teacher.* Ed. Carolyn Keefe. 1971. Grand Rapids, MI: Zondervan, 1980. 37–62.

Hopkins, Gerard. "Charles Williams 1886–1945." *Supplement to "The Periodical"* July 1945. Rpt. of article in *The Bookseller* 2059 (24 May 1945). Oxford: Oxford University Press, 1945: i–iv.

Howard, Thomas. *The Novels of Charles Williams.* New York: Oxford University Press, 1983.

Huttar, Charles A. "A Lifelong Love Affair with Language: C. S. Lewis's Poetry." *Word and Story in C. S. Lewis.* Ed. Peter J. Schakel and Charles A. Huttar. Columbia: University of Missouri Press, 1991. 86–108.

Jones, Siriol Hugh. "Vogue's Spotlight." *Vogue.* Apr. 1947: 75+.

J. R. R. Tolkien: An Audio Portrait. Presented by Brian Sibley. BBC Worldwide Ltd., 2001.

Kilby, Clyde S. *Tolkien and The Silmarillion.* Wheaton, IL: Harold Shaw, 1976.

King, Don W. *C. S. Lewis, Poet: The Legacy of His Poetic Impulse.* Kent, OH: Kent State University Press, 2001.

King, Roma A., Jr., *The Pattern in the Web: The Mythical Poetry of Charles Williams.* Kent, OH: Kent State University Press, 1990.

Knight, Gareth. *The Magical World of the Inklings: J. R. R. Tolkien, C. S. Lewis, Charles Williams, Owen Barfield.* Longmead, England: Element Books, 1990.

Lasswell, Harold D. "The Social Setting of Creativity." *Creativity and Its Cultivation.* Ed. Harold H. Anderson. New York: Harper & Brothers, 1959. 203–21.

LeFevre, Karen Burke. *Invention as a Social Act.* Carbondale: Southern Illinois University Press, 1987.

Lewis, C. S. *The Allegory of Love: A Study in Medieval Tradition*. 1936. Oxford: Oxford University Press, 1985.

———. *All My Road Before Me: The Diary of C. S. Lewis 1922–1927*. Ed. Walter Hooper. San Diego: Harcourt Brace Jovanovich, 1991.

———. *Beyond Personality: The Christian Idea of God*. London: Bles-Centenary Press, 1944.

———. *Boxen: The Imaginary World of the Young C. S. Lewis*. Ed. Walter Hooper. New York: Harcourt Brace Jovanovich, 1985.

———. *C. S. Lewis' Lost Aeneid: Arms and the Exile*. Ed. A. T. Reyes. New Haven, CT: Yale University Press, 2011.

———. "Charles Walter Stansby Williams (1886–1945)." Obituary. *Oxford Magazine*. 24 May 1945: 265.

———. *Christian Behaviour*. 1943. London: Bles-Centenary Press, 1946.

———. *Christian Reflections*. 1967. Ed. Walter Hooper. Grand Rapids, MI: Eerdmans, 1989.

———. *Collected Letters*. Ed. Walter Hooper. 3 vol. London: HarperCollins, 2000–2006.

———. *The Collected Poems of C. S. Lewis*. Ed. Walter Hooper. London: Fount-HarperCollins, 1994.

———. *The Discarded Image: An Introduction to Medieval and Renaissance Literature*. 1964. Cambridge: Cambridge University Press, 1967.

———. *Dymer*. 1926. *Narrative Poems*. Ed. Walter Hooper. New York: Harcourt Brace Jovanovich, 1969. 1–91.

———. *English Literature in the Sixteenth Century, excluding Drama*. 1954. Oxford History of English Literature 3. Oxford: Oxford University Press, 1973.

———. Preface. *Essays Presented to Charles Williams*. 1947. Grand Rapids, MI: Eerdmans, 1966. v-xiv.

———. *An Experiment in Criticism*. 1961. Cambridge: Cambridge University Press, 1988.

———. *The Four Loves*. 1960. San Diego: Harvest-Harcourt, 1988.

———. *The Great Divorce*. 1945. New York: Touchstone-Simon & Schuster, 1996.

———. "The Hobbit." *On Stories and Other Essays on Literature*. 81–82.

———. "Letter to Edmund Meškys, 3 October 1963." *Niekas* 7 (15 December 1963): 23.

———. *Letters of C. S. Lewis*. Ed. and with a Memoir by W. H. Lewis. 1966. Rev. and enl. ed. Walter Hooper. San Diego: Harcourt Brace, 1988.

———. *Letters to an American Lady*. Ed. Clyde S. Kilby. Grand Rapids, MI: Eerdmans, 1967.

———. *Letters to Malcolm: Chiefly on Prayer*. New York: Harcourt Brace and World, 1964.

———. *The Lion, the Witch and the Wardrobe*. 1950. New York: Harper Trophy-HarperCollins, 1994.

———. *The Magician's Nephew.* New York: Macmillan, 1955.

———. *Mere Christianity: A revised and enlarged edition, with a new introduction, of the three books The Case for Christianity, Christian Behaviour, and Beyond Personality.* 1952. First paperback ed. New York: Collier-Macmillan, 1960.

———. *Miracles: A Preliminary Study.* 1947. Rev. 1960. New York: Harper-SanFrancisco-HarperCollins, 2001.

———. "Myth Became Fact." *God in the Dock: Essays on Theology and Ethics.* Ed. Walter Hooper. Grand Rapids, MI: Eerdmans, 1970. 63–67.

———. *On Stories and Other Essays on Literature.* Ed. Walter Hooper. New York: Harvest-Harcourt Brace, 1982.

———. *Out of the Silent Planet.* 1938. New York: Macmillan, 1965.

———. *Perelandra: A Novel.* 1943. New York: Scribner Paperback Fiction-Simon and Schuster, 1996.

———. *The Pilgrim's Regress: An Allegorical Apology for Christianity, Reason, and Romanticism.* 1933. Grand Rapids, MI: Eerdmans, 1981.

———. *Poems.* Ed. Walter Hooper. New York: Harcourt Brace Jovanovich, 1964.

———. *Present Concerns.* Ed. Walter Hooper. San Diego: Harcourt Brace Jovanovich, 1986.

———. *Prince Caspian: The Return to Narnia.* 1951. New York: Collier-Macmillan, 1975.

———. *The Problem of Pain.* 1940. Appendix R. Havard. New York: Macmillan, 1944.

———. "Professor Tolkien's 'Hobbit.'" Rev. of *The Hobbit. The Times.* 8 Oct. 1937: 20.

———. *Reflections on the Psalms.* New York: Harcourt Brace Jovanovich, 1958.

———. *Rehabilitations and Other Essays.* London: Oxford University Press, 1939.

———. "A Reply to Professor Haldane." *On Stories and Other Essays on Literature.* 69–79.

———. "A Sacred Poem." Rev. of *Taliessin Through Logres,* by Charles Williams. *Theology* 38 (1939): 268–76.

———. *The Screwtape Letters: with Screwtape Proposes a Toast.* 1942; 1961. New York: HarperSanFrancisco-HarperCollins, 2001.

———. *Selected Literary Essays.* 1969. Ed. Walter Hooper. Cambridge: Cambridge University Press, 1980.

———. *The Silver Chair.* New York: Macmillan, 1953.

———. *Studies in Words.* 1960. 2nd ed. Cambridge: Cambridge University Press, 1967.

———. *Surprised by Joy: The Shape of My Early Life.* New York: Harcourt, Brace and World, 1955.

———. Rev. of *Taliessin Through Logres,* by Charles Williams. *Oxford Magazine* 14 Mar. 1946: 248–50.

——. *That Hideous Strength: A Modern Fairy-Tale for Grown-Ups.* 1946. New York: Collier-Macmillan, 1965.

——. *They Stand Together: The Letters of C. S. Lewis to Arthur Greeves (1914–1963).* Ed. Walter Hooper. New York: Macmillan, 1979.

——. *Till We Have Faces: A Myth Retold.* 1956. New York: Harcourt Brace, 1985.

——. "Tolkien's *The Lord of the Rings.*" *On Stories and Other Essays on Literature.* 83–90.

——. *The Tortured Planet.* Abr. ed. of *That Hideous Strength.* New York: Avon Publications, 1946.

——. *The Voyage of the "Dawn Treader."* New York: Macmillan, 1952.

——. *Voyage to Venus.* Abr. ed. of *Perelandra.* 1943. London: Pan Books. 1953.

——. *The Weight of Glory and Other Addresses.* 1949. Grand Rapids, MI: Eerdmans, 1979.

Lewis, C. S., and Dorothy L. Sayers. "Charles Williams." Letter. *Times* [London] 14 May 1955: 9.

Lewis, Warren Hamilton. *Assault on Olympus: The Rise of the House of Gramont between 1604 and 1678.* New York: Harcourt, Brace, 1958.

——. *Brothers and Friends: The Diaries of Major Warren Hamilton Lewis.* Ed. Clyde S. Kilby and Marjorie Lamp Mead. San Francisco: Harper and Row, 1982.

——. *The Splendid Century: Life in the France of Louis XIV.* 1953. New York: Doubleday, 1957.

——. *The Sunset of the Splendid Century: The Life and Times of Louis Auguste de Bourbon, Duc du Maine 1670–1736.* 1955. New York: Doubleday, 1963.

Lindsay, David. *A Voyage to Arcturus.* 1920. Lincoln: University of Nebraska Press, 2002.

Long, Josh B. "Disparaging Narnia: Reconsidering Tolkien's View of Lewis's *The Lion, the Witch and the Wardrobe.*" *Mythlore* 31.3/4. (whole number 121/122 Spring/Summer 2013): 31–46.

Mathew, Gervase. *The Court of Richard II.* London: Murray, 1968.

——. "Justice and Charity in *The Vision of Piers Plowman.*" *Dominican Studies* 1 (1948): 360–66.

——. "Williams and the Arthuriad." Rev. of *Arthurian Torso* by Charles Williams and C. S. Lewis. *Time and Tide* 1 Jan. 1949: 14.

Mitchell, Christopher W. "Bearing the Weight of Glory: The Cost of C. S. Lewis's Witness." *The Pilgrim's Guide: C. S. Lewis and the Art of Witness.* Ed. David Mills. Grand Rapids, MI: Eerdman's, 1998. 3–14.

Morgan, Edwin. Rev. of *The Sunset of the Splendid Century* by Warren Lewis. *America* 31 Dec. 1955: 383.

Morris, Clifford. "A Christian Gentleman." *Como* 317–30.

Oakeshott, Michael. "The Voice of Poetry in the Conversation of Mankind." *Rationalism in Politics.* New York: Basic Books, 1962. 197–247.

Phillips, Justin. *C. S. Lewis at the BBC: Messages of Hope in the Darkness of War*. London: HarperCollins, 2003.

Plimmer, Charlotte, and Denis Plimmer. "The Man Who Understands Hobbits." *London Daily Telegraph Magazine* March 1968: 31+.

Rogers, Mary. "Rejected by Oxford." *Oxford Today: The University Magazine*. Michaelmas 1998: 53–55.

Sawyer, Keith. *Group Genius: The Creative Power of Collaboration*. New York: Basic Books, 2007.

Sayer, George. *Jack: C. S. Lewis and His Times*. San Francisco: Harper and Row, 1988.

———. "Recollections of J. R. R. Tolkien." *Proceedings of the J. R. R. Tolkien Centenary Conference 1992*. Eds. Patricia Reynolds and Glen GoodKnight. Milton Keynes and Altadena, CA: Tolkien Society, Mythopoeic Press, 1995. 21–25.

Sayers, Dorothy L. *Further Papers on Dante*. New York: Harper and Brothers, 1957.

Shenk, Joshua Wolf. *Powers of Two: Finding the Essence of Innovation in Creative Pairs*. Boston: Houghton Mifflin Harcourt, 2014.

Shippey, Tom. *Beyond the Movie: The Lord of the Rings: The Fellowship of the Ring*. Dir. Lisa Kors. *National Geographic*, 2002.

———. *J. R. R. Tolkien: Author of the Century*. Boston: Houghton Mifflin, 2002.

Simmons, Michael. "If You Want To Go Fast, Go Alone. If You Want To Go Far, Go Together." http://www.forbes.com. Accessed 20 Feb 2015.

Starr, Nathan C. "Good Cheer and Sustenance." *Como* 219–26.

Tennyson, G. B., ed. and Introduction. *Owen Barfield on C. S. Lewis*. Middletown, CT: Wesleyan University Press, 1989. xi–xx.

Tillyard, E. M. W., and C. S. Lewis. *The Personal Heresy: A Controversy*. 1939. London: Oxford University Press, 1965.

Tolkien, Christopher, ed. *The History of Middle-earth*. By J. R. R. Tolkien. 12 vols. Boston: Houghton Mifflin, 1983–96.

———. Foreword. *The Hobbit: or There and Back Again*. By J. R. R. Tolkien. Special 50th Anniversary Ed. 1987. Boston: Houghton Mifflin, 1966. N. pag.

———. 'Notes on the Pictures.' *J. R. R. Tolkien Calendar 1979*. London: Allen & Unwin, 1978.

———. 'Notes on the Pictures.' *The Lord of the Rings 1977 Calendar*. London: Allen & Unwin, 1976.

———. Foreword and notes. *Pictures by J. R. R. Tolkien*. 1979. Boston: Houghton Mifflin, 1992. N. pag.

———. 'Notes on the Pictures.' *The Silmarillion Calendar 1978*. London: Allen & Unwin, 1977.

———. *The Silmarillion [by] J. R. R. Tolkien: A Brief Account of the Book and Its Making*. Boston: Houghton Mifflin, 1977.

————. Introduction. *Tree and Leaf Including the Poem Mythopoeia*. By J. R. R. Tolkien. Boston: Houghton Mifflin, 1989. 5–8.

Tolkien, John, and Priscilla Tolkien. *The Tolkien Family Album*. Boston: Houghton Mifflin, 1992.

Tolkien, J. R. R. *The Adventures of Tom Bombadil: and other verses from The Red Book*. Boston: Houghton Mifflin, 1962.

————. "*Beowulf*: The Monsters and the Critics." 1936. *The Monsters and the Critics and Other Essays*. 5–48.

————. *Beowulf: A Translation and Commentary, together with Sellic Spell*. Boston: Houghton Mifflin Harcourt, 2014.

————. *Bilbo's Last Song (at the Grey Havens)*. 1974. Rev. ed. New York: Knopf, 2002.

————. "Chaucer as a Philologist: The Reeve's Tale." *Transactions of the Philological Society*. London: David Nutt, 1934: 1–70.

————. *The Children of Húrin*. Ed. Christopher Tolkien. Boston: Houghton Mifflin, 2007.

————. "English and Welsh." 1963. *The Monsters and the Critics and Other Essays*. 162–97.

————. *The Fall of Arthur*. Ed. Christopher Tolkien. Boston: Houghton Mifflin, 2013.

————. *Farmer Giles of Ham*. 1949. London: Allen & Unwin, 1966.

————. *The Fellowship of the Ring: Being the first part of The Lord of the Rings*. 1954. Boston: Houghton Mifflin, 1994.

————. *The Hobbit: or There and Back Again*. Foreword. Christopher Tolkien. Special 50th Anniversary Ed. 1987. Boston: Houghton Mifflin, 1966.

————. *The Lays of Beleriand. The History of Middle-earth* 3. Ed. Christopher Tolkien. Boston: Houghton Mifflin, 1985.

————. "Leaf by Niggle." 1945. *Tree and Leaf*. 75–95.

————. *The Legend of Sigurd & Gudrún*. Ed. Christopher Tolkien. Boston: Houghton Mifflin, 2009.

————. *The Letters of J. R. R. Tolkien*. Ed. Humphrey Carpenter with the assistance of Christopher Tolkien. Boston: Houghton Mifflin, 2000.

————. *The Lord of the Rings*. One Volume Edition. Boston: Houghton Mifflin, 1994.

————. *The Lost Road and Other Writings: Language and Legend before 'The Lord of the Rings.' The History of Middle-earth* 5. Ed. Christopher Tolkien. Boston: Houghton Mifflin, 1987.

————. *A Middle English Vocabulary: Fourteenth Century Verse and Prose*. 1922. Ed. Kenneth Sissam. Oxford: Clarendon Press, 1946. N. pag.

————. *The Monsters and the Critics and Other Essays*. Ed. Christopher Tolkien. London: Allen & Unwin, 1983.

————. *Mr. Bliss*. Boston: Houghton Mifflin, 1983.

———. "Mythopoeia." *Tree and Leaf.* 97–101.

———. "The Notion Club Papers." *Sauron Defeated.* 143–327.

———. "On Fairy Stories." *Tree and Leaf.* 9–73.

———. *The Return of the King: Being the third part of The Lord of the Rings.* 1955. Boston: Houghton Mifflin, 1994.

———. *The Return of the Shadow: The History of The Lord of the Rings Part One. The History of Middle-earth* 6. Ed. Christopher Tolkien. Boston: Houghton Mifflin, 1988.

———. *Roverandom.* Boston: Houghton Mifflin, 1998.

———. *Sauron Defeated: The End of the Third Age (The History of The Lord of the Rings Part Four). The History of Middle-earth* 9. Ed. Christopher Tolkien. London: HarperCollins, 1992.

———. *The Silmarillion.* Ed. Christopher Tolkien. Boston: Houghton Mifflin, 1977.

———, trans. *Sir Gawain and the Green Knight, Pearl, and Sir Orfeo.* Ed. and Preface. Christopher Tolkien. Boston: Houghton Mifflin, 1975.

———. *Smith of Wootton Major.* Boston: Houghton Mifflin, 1967.

———. *The Treason of Isengard: The History of The Lord of the Rings Part Two. The History of Middle-earth* 7. Ed. Christopher Tolkien. Boston: Houghton Mifflin, 1989.

———. *Tree and Leaf Including the poem Mythopoeia.* 1964. Intr. Christopher Tolkien. Boston: Houghton Mifflin, 1989.

———. *Unfinished Tales of Númenor and Middle-earth.* Ed. Christopher Tolkien. Boston: Houghton Mifflin, 1980.

———. *The War of the Ring: The History of The Lord of the Rings Part Three. The History of Middle-earth* 8. Ed. Christopher Tolkien. Boston: Houghton Mifflin, 1990.

Tyler, J. E. A. *The New Tolkien Companion.* 2nd. ed. 1st rev. printing. New York: Avon, 1980.

Unwin, Rayner. "Early Days of Elder Days." Flieger and Hostetter 3–6.

Wain, John. *Arnold Bennett.* Columbia Essays on Modern Writers 23. Irvington, NY: Columbia University Press, 1967.

———. "A Great Clerke." *Como* 152–63.

———. "John Wain." *Contemporary Authors.* Autobiography Series 4. Detroit, MI: Gale Research, 1986. 314–32.

———. *Mixed Feelings: Nineteen Poems.* Reading: University of Reading, 1951.

———. *Sprightly Running: Part of an Autobiography.* New York: St Martin's Press, 1963.

Walsh, Chad. *C. S. Lewis: Apostle to the Skeptics.* New York: Macmillan, 1949.

West, Richard C. "W. H. Lewis: Historian of the Inklings and of Seventeenth-Century France." *Seven: An Anglo-American Literary Review* 14 (1997): 75–86.

Wheeler, Helen Tyrrell. "Wartime Tutor." Graham 48–52.

Williams, Charles. *All Hallows' Eve.* 1945. Grand Rapids, MI: Eerdmans, 1981.

———. *The Arthurian Poems of Charles Williams: Taliessin Through Logres and The Region of the Summer Stars.* Woodbridge, England: D. S. Brewer-Boydell and Brewer, 1982.

———. *Descent Into Hell.* 1937. Grand Rapids, MI: Eerdmans, 1980.

———. *The Descent of the Dove: A History of the Holy Spirit in the Church.* 1939. New York: Meridian, 1956.

———. "The Figure of Arthur." *Arthurian Torso: containing the posthumous fragment of The Figure of Arthur by Charles Williams and a Commentary on the Arthurian Poems of Charles Williams by C. S. Lewis.* 1948. London: Oxford University Press, 1969.

———. *He Came Down from Heaven.* 1938. Grand Rapids, MI: Eerdmans, 1984.

———. "Letters in Hell." Rev. of *The Screwtape Letters,* by C. S. Lewis. *Time and Tide* 21 Mar. 1942: 245–46.

———. *Letters to Lalage: The Letters of Charles Williams to Lois Lang-Sims.* Kent, OH: Kent State University Press, 1989.

———. "The Noises that Weren't There." *Mythlore* 2.2 (whole no. 6 Autumn 1970): 17–21; 2.3 (no. 7 Winter 1971): 17–23; 2.4 (no. 8 Winter 1972): 21–25.

———. *The Place of the Lion.* 1931. Grand Rapids, MI: Eerdmans, 1980.

———. Rev. of *The Problem of Pain,* by C. S. Lewis. *Theology* 42 (Jan. 1941): 62–63.

———. Rev. of *The Screwtape Letters,* by C. S. Lewis. *Dublin Review* 211 (1942): 170–71.

———. *Seed of Adam.* 1948. *Collected Plays.* Ed. John Heath-Stubbs. London: Oxford University Press, 1963. 149–75.

———. *Terror of Light. Collected Plays.* Ed. John Heath-Stubbs. London: Oxford University Press, 1963. 325–74.

———. *To Michal from Serge: Letters from Charles Williams to His Wife, Florence, 1939–1945.* Ed. Roma A. King, Jr. Kent, OH: Kent State University Press, 2002.

Williams, Charles, and C. S. Lewis. *Arthurian Torso: containing the posthumous fragment of The Figure of Arthur by Charles Williams and a Commentary on the Arthurian Poems of Charles Williams by C. S. Lewis.* London: Oxford University Press, 1969.

Wilson, A. N. *C. S. Lewis: A Biography.* New York: Norton, 1990.

Wrenn, C. L., ed. *Beowulf, with the Finnesburg Fragment.* London: Harrap, 1953.

———. *A Study of Old English Literature.* London: Harrap, 1967.

Index

Works by the Inklings are indexed under title.

Abbreviations: CSL (C. S. Lewis), CT (Christopher Tolkien), CW (Charles Williams), JRRT (J. R. R. Tolkien), LOTR (*The Lord of the Rings*, by JRRT), OB (Owen Barfield), WHL (Warren Lewis)

About the Author

Diana Pavlac Glyer thinks that studying faded pencil marks on manuscripts is much more fun than going to Disneyland. That's why she has spent more than 40 years combing through archives and lurking in libraries. She is a leading expert on C. S. Lewis, J. R. R. Tolkien, and the Inklings; her award-winning book *The Company They Keep* changed the way we talk about these writers. Her scholarship, her teaching, and her work as an artist all circle back to one common theme: creativity thrives in community.

About the Illustrator

James A. Owen has written and illustrated the *Starchild* graphic novel, the *Mythworld* series of novels, the best-selling *The Chronicles of the Imaginarium Geographica,* and the forthcoming series *Fool's Hollow.* He is also the author of the inspirational nonfiction trilogy *The Meditations* and the illustrator/designer of *The Hundred Books Project,* a series that showcases some of the greatest books ever published. His books have been translated into more than twenty languages, and more than a million copies are in print. He works in the Coppervale Studio, a century-old restored church in Northeastern Arizona.